Project 2025 - A Chilling Blueprint for Authoritarian Rule

Unmasking the Conservative Plan to Reshape America and Empowering Citizens to Safeguard Their Freedoms

William Chandler

Publisher: [William Chandler]Edition: 2024

Introduction

Shouldn't progress mean equality for ALL, not just a select few? Shouldn't an honest America be an OPEN America, with room for ALL voices? These pressing questions echo through the corridors of our collective consciousness, urging us to scrutinize Project 2025 and its implications. What happens when the foundational pillars of democracy—liberty, equality, and justice—are threatened by policies that claim to restore greatness but risk fostering division and inequality? This book is your call to action, your guide through the labyrinthine political landscape where the stakes have never been higher.

Project 2025, heralded by some as a return to a 'greater' America, poses significant risks to the democratic principles we cherish. It is not merely a policy blueprint; it is a vision that could reshape the very fabric of our nation in ways that may stifle diversity, silence dissenting voices, and erode hard-won freedoms. The urgency to understand and confront this initiative cannot be overstated. If left unchallenged, Project 2025 threatens to dismantle the democratic ideals that underpin our society, replacing them with a governance model that prioritizes exclusion over inclusion.

This is not just another political critique; it is a vital exploration into the heart of what makes our democracy resilient and what can render it vulnerable. Imagine living in a country where essential services are stripped away, where the voices of the most vulnerable are silenced and forgotten, leaving families to navigate a harsh reality alone. Picture a scenario where environmental protections are rolled back, exacerbating climate crises that disproportionately affect marginalized communities. Visualize a future where social justice initiatives grind to a halt, deepening the chasm between the privileged and the oppressed.

These are not distant possibilities but imminent threats that need immediate attention. Through well-researched insights and compelling narratives, this book aims to shed light on the multifaceted dangers posed by Project 2025. Our journey will take us through critical analyses of policy proposals, detailed examinations of their potential impacts, and strategies for grassroots advocacy and resistance.

To the politically active individuals who identify with progressive or liberal ideologies, this book is your toolkit. You seek to understand the roots of authoritarian trends that threaten to unravel the social progress we've fought so hard to achieve. Here, you will find the knowledge and strategies needed to counteract these dangerous trends effectively. Your passion for equitable change, coupled with informed activism, is crucial in protecting our democracy from regressive forces.

For academics, political analysts, and students of political science or public policy, this book serves as a comprehensive resource. It delves into the complexities of Project 2025, providing thorough examinations necessary for research, analysis, and education. The nuanced perspectives offered here will enhance your understanding of contemporary political movements, equipping you with the analytical tools needed to contribute meaningfully to scholarly and public discourses on governance and democracy.

Environmental activists and social justice advocates, your causes stand at a critical juncture. The conservative policies proposed under Project 2025 have far-reaching implications for both the environment and marginalized communities. This book offers insights that will help you grasp the scope of these challenges and engage in strategic resistance. Armed with information, you can better advocate for sustainable and inclusive policies that protect both our planet and the rights of those often pushed to their fringes.

Our analysis begins with a deep dive into the origins and ideological underpinnings of Project 2025. We will trace the historical context that has shaped current political dynamics, uncovering the motivations behind this initiative. By understanding the past, we gain clarity on how to navigate the future. This foundational knowledge sets the stage for more detailed explorations of specific policy areas affected by Project 2025, from healthcare and education to immigration and labor rights.

A critical examination of the project's environmental policies will reveal how regulatory rollbacks and corporate favoritism threaten ecological balance and community health. We will explore case studies illustrating the localized impact of these policies, drawing connections to broader global environmental issues. Similarly, our investigation into social justice implications will highlight how marginalized groups bear the brunt of regressive policies, reinforcing systemic inequalities and hindering social mobility.

Throughout this book, personal stories and scenarios will bring these issues to life, connecting abstract policies to real-world consequences. These narratives serve as powerful reminders of what is at stake, emphasizing the human element often overlooked in political debates. They will illustrate the resilience and struggle of those fighting against oppressive systems, inspiring readers to join the cause with renewed vigor.

In addition to providing a detailed critique, this book also aims to empower readers with actionable strategies for resistance. Grassroots advocacy is a potent force in shaping public opinion and influencing policy changes. We will explore successful models of grassroots movements, offering practical advice on organizing, mobilizing, and sustaining efforts for impactful resistance. Whether it's through community engagement, digital activism, or coalition-building, this book equips you with the tools to make a difference.

Ultimately, the purpose of this book is clear: to inform, empower, and equip. By exposing the hidden dangers of Project 2025, we aim to galvanize a broad coalition of concerned citizens committed to defending democratic values and promoting a just and sustainable future. This is a call to action for everyone who believes in an open, inclusive, and equitable America.

As we embark on this journey together, remember that knowledge is power. Understanding the intricacies of Project 2025 enables us to challenge its premises and propose alternative visions rooted in equity and justice. By critically engaging with the content presented here, you become an integral part of a movement striving for a better, fairer future. Let's rise to the occasion, armed with insight and driven by a shared commitment to safeguarding our democracy and protecting our planet for generations to come.

Chapter 1: Introduction to Project 2025

Project 2025 represents a bold and contentious initiative designed to reshape the federal government and societal structures, presenting a comprehensive conservative agenda that has far-reaching implications for American democracy. This chapter critically examines the foundational elements of Project 2025, offering an analytical assessment of its goals and objectives. It delves into the ambitious proposals set forth by the project, scrutinizing their potential impacts on democratic institutions, civil liberties, and social equity. By evaluating these proposals in detail, the chapter aims to provide a nuanced understanding of how this initiative could fundamentally alter the political landscape.

The chapter also explores the initial reactions from various sectors, shedding light on the diverse spectrum of public and political responses to Project 2025. From widespread public outcry and grassroots mobilizations to the polarized views within political and scholarly circles, the introduction of Project 2025 has triggered significant debate and activism. By examining these early reactions, the chapter highlights the contentious nature of the project's objectives and offers insights into the broader socio-political dynamics at play. Readers will gain a thorough understanding of the initial response landscape, setting the stage for a deeper analysis of the project's implications and potential outcomes.

Goals and Objectives of Project 2025

Project 2025 is an ambitious initiative that outlines a sweeping conservative agenda aimed at transforming the federal government and society. The project's primary intentions pose significant risks to democratic values and civil liberties, which makes it imperative to delve into its key components.

The policy agenda of Project 2025 involves several major proposals with far-reaching consequences. Among these are initiatives aimed at consolidating power within the executive branch, raising costs for middle-class families, and undermining civil rights protections. For example, one proposal calls for reclassifying tens of thousands of civil servants as political appointees, stripping them of labor protections, and enabling the president to replace them with loyalists (Radosevich et al., 2024). This drastic measure could erode the independence of crucial public agencies and weaken the checks and balances that are fundamental to American democracy.

Another critical aspect of Project 2025's policy agenda includes initiatives that threaten individual freedoms and increase socioeconomic disparities. Proposals to restrict access to contraception and raise the cost of prescription drugs would disproportionately affect vulnerable populations, thereby exacerbating social inequality (Radosevich et al., 2024). Additionally, slashing funding for early childhood education and K-12 schools poses severe risks to the future workforce, potentially resulting in long-term economic stagnation.

The long-term aspirations driving Project 2025 are even more concerning. The ultimate goal appears to be a shift toward authoritarian governance under the guise of reform. By consolidating power in the presidency and weakening independent agencies such as the FBI and the Department of Justice, the administration would gain unprecedented control over law enforcement and regulatory bodies. This centralization of authority not only undermines democratic principles but also opens the door for potential abuses of power. For instance, Project 2025 would give the president the ability to investigate and prosecute political opponents using federal resources, further entrenching authoritarian rule (Radosevich et al., 2024).

Exploring the interconnectedness of various policies within Project 2025 reveals a deliberate strategy that enhances the likelihood of their implementation. Each policy is designed not only to stand alone but also to support others within the broader agenda. For instance, by reducing funding for public education while simultaneously curbing civil rights protections, Project 2025 creates a scenario where marginalized communities have diminished opportunities for upward mobility and less legal recourse to challenge discriminatory practices. This interconnected approach ensures that each regressive policy reinforces the others, leading to a cumulative impact that strengthens authoritarian control.

The social and economic implications of Project 2025 are vast and troubling. From a social perspective, the proposed policies stand to deepen divisions within American society. Cutting programs like Head Start and educational funding disproportionately affects low-income families, amplifying existing inequalities (Radosevich et al., 2024). Moreover, dismantling civil rights protections exposes minority communities to heightened discrimination and systemic injustices, further polarizing the nation.

Economically, the ramifications could prove devastating. Increasing mortgage insurance premiums and making healthcare more expensive for those with preexisting conditions place additional financial burdens on already struggling households. These measures could lead to increased poverty rates and reduced consumer spending, destabilizing local economies. On a national level, the concentration of wealth facilitated by lower corporate taxes and deregulation favors the rich, widening the gap between the wealthy and the middle class and undermining overall economic stability (Radosevich et al., 2024).

One illustrative example of the broader societal effects can be seen in the environmental arena. Project 2025's plans to halt action against climate change not only risk environmental degradation but also jeopardize public health and safety. Geographic regions already vulnerable to climate impacts could face intensified natural disasters, forcing communities to deal with long-term economic disruptions and health crises.

Initial Reactions from the Public

Project 2025 has elicited strong reactions from various stakeholders, providing a rich landscape for examining public perception and political discourse. In this subpoint, we explore the multifaceted responses, focusing on the immediate public outcry, grassroots mobilizations, the scale of public response, and policy awareness among the general populace.

Public Outcry

The announcement of Project 2025 led to immediate widespread concern, particularly regarding its implications for civil rights and liberties. Across the nation, citizens expressed fears about the potential erosion of democratic norms, with significant anxieties surrounding the suggested increase in government intrusion into private lives. This sentiment was not isolated but rather echoed by numerous advocacy groups and think tanks. Such concerns focused on proposals like deploying the military for domestic law enforcement, arresting and deporting undocumented immigrants, and restricting access to reproductive healthcare (Walker, n.d.). These drastic measures sparked intense debates, often painting a grim picture of the future under such policies.

Public protests became commonplace, with demonstrators decrying what they perceived as regressive steps that would dismantle hard-won rights for marginalized communities. The conversation quickly moved online as well, with social media becoming a battleground for fiery debates on the project's potential ramifications. High-profile figures and influencers used their platforms to amplify these issues, propelling them into the national spotlight and ensuring that Project 2025 remained a dominant topic of discussion long after its announcement.

Grassroots Mobilizations

In response to the alarming aspects of Project 2025, grassroots movements have sprung into action across the country. Activists and community organizers have been at the forefront of these efforts, drawing attention to the threats posed by the project and rallying support against it. Demonstrations, featuring speeches and marches, have been pivotal in raising awareness and garnering opposition to prevent its implementation.

Events like panel discussions and film festivals have also played a significant role in educating the public and mobilizing resistance. For example, in Houston, local activists organized gatherings aimed at informing marginalized communities about the potential impacts of Project 2025 and outlining strategies to combat these changes. These events not only provided information but also fostered a sense of solidarity and shared purpose among participants.

Grassroots mobilizations have also utilized digital tools to coordinate efforts, spreading their message more efficiently and galvanizing broader participation. Platforms such as Facebook,

Twitter, and WhatsApp have been instrumental in organizing events, sharing resources, and creating networks of engaged citizens who are ready to act.

Scale of Public Response

To understand the long-term civic engagement with Project 2025, it's crucial to assess the extent of the public outcry. Initial responses were robust, with large-scale protests and widespread media coverage highlighting the contentious nature of the project. However, measuring the sustained impact of this reaction involves looking at several factors, including continued participation in protests, ongoing discussions in both mainstream and alternative media, and the evolution of grassroots initiatives over time.

Surveys and polls conducted soon after the announcement revealed that a significant portion of the population was deeply concerned about the project's implications. These findings offered a snapshot of the prevailing public mood and set the stage for further analysis of how these sentiments might translate into prolonged civic engagement.

Policy Awareness

A critical aspect of understanding the public's response to Project 2025 is gauging their awareness of the policy details and their potential impacts on daily life. While initial reactions were driven by broad concerns, deeper insights can be gleaned by examining how thoroughly the public grasps the specific elements of the project.

Research indicates that while there is a general apprehension about the overarching themes of the project, many individuals lack detailed knowledge about its specific proposals. Efforts by activists and educators to bridge this gap are essential for fostering informed discourse. Educational campaigns, town hall meetings, and media programs play vital roles in unpacking the complexities of the project and making them accessible to a wider audience.

For instance, the abolition of the Department of Education and the redirection of scientific research funding to only align with conservative principles are nuanced topics that require careful explanation. By illustrating how these changes could affect everyday life—such as alterations to school curriculums or shifts in research priorities—activists can help the public understand the stakes involved more comprehensively.

Examining the response to Project 2025 through the lenses of public outcry, grassroots mobilizations, the scale of public response, and policy awareness reveals a dynamic and evolving landscape of civic engagement. Each of these elements provides valuable insights into how different stakeholders perceive and react to this controversial initiative.

The initial public outcry underscores the profound concerns many have about the direction of government policies and their impact on civil rights. Grassroots mobilizations highlight the proactive steps taken by communities to resist and educate others about the potential dangers. Assessing the scale of the response offers a gauge of long-term engagement while examining policy awareness emphasizes the importance of an informed citizenry in shaping effective opposition.

Political and Scholarly Engagement

Project 2025 has become a polarizing topic within political circles and academic discourse. This analysis delves into how it is framed within these spheres, ultimately shaping public understanding and political strategies.

Political Polarization

The reactions from political leaders to Project 2025 are starkly divided. On one side, conservative figures endorse the initiatives laid out in Project 2025, heralding it as a necessary recalibration of government policies to restore traditional values and national pride. They argue that it addresses pressing issues such as economic stagnation and national security, framing it as a pivotal move towards a stronger, more unified nation. On the other hand, progressive leaders vehemently oppose the project, citing it as a dangerous shift towards authoritarianism that threatens democratic norms and institutions. They warn that Project 2025 could result in the erosion of civil liberties, increased inequality, and greater social divisions. This polarized reception underscores a significant ideological rift, reflecting broader trends of political polarization in American politics.

Media Framing

Media representation plays a critical role in shaping public perception of Project 2025. Mainstream media outlets often present the project through a lens of skepticism or outright criticism, emphasizing potential risks and negative outcomes. Reports frequently highlight expert warnings and public dissent, painting a picture of a contentious and controversial initiative. Alternative media, however, may provide a more favorable portrayal, aligning with conservative viewpoints and underscoring the project's alleged benefits. These outlets might focus on success stories, endorsements by key political figures, and theoretical gains for national strength and unity. Such contrasting narratives reveal inherent biases in media coverage, which can significantly influence public opinion based on the sources they trust. The divergent media framing illustrates how interpretive lenses can magnify or minimize perceived threats and benefits associated with Project 2025, contributing to public debates and reinforcing existing partisan divides (Coan, 2024).

Expert Analysis

Scholarly responses to Project 2025 have been predominantly critical, sounding alarms about the project's implications for democracy. Political scientists and constitutional experts express concern over the proposed changes to governmental structures, fearing they could centralize power and undermine checks and balances essential for a functioning democracy. Legal scholars worry about potential infringements on civil rights and liberties, particularly relating to freedoms of speech, assembly, and the press. Economists critique the project's economic policies, predicting adverse effects on social equity and long-term financial stability. These expert critiques suggest that Project 2025 could pave the way for authoritarian governance under the guise of reform, raising red flags that warrant serious consideration by policymakers and the public alike. The scholarly consensus emphasizes the need for vigilant oversight and robust debate to safeguard democratic principles against encroachment (Berman, 2024).

Academic Discourse

The academic community offers several critical frameworks to enhance public understanding and engagement with Project 2025. One approach involves examining the historical context of similar political movements, drawing parallels with past instances where extensive governmental reforms led to increased authoritarian control. This comparative analysis aids in recognizing potential warning signs and understanding the conditions under which such projects gain traction. Another framework focuses on the socio-political dynamics that foster support for Project 2025, exploring factors such as economic uncertainty, cultural anxieties, and populist rhetoric. By identifying these underlying drivers, academics aim to demystify the appeal of the project and highlight areas for constructive intervention. Additionally, interdisciplinary studies that incorporate perspectives from sociology, psychology, and communication studies offer a holistic view of how Project 2025 affects societal cohesion and individual behavior. These comprehensive analyses equip the public with nuanced insights that facilitate informed civic participation and advocacy (Coan, 2024).

Chapter 2: The Conservative Ideology Behind the Blueprint

Understanding the conservative ideology behind Project 2025 is crucial for grasping its blueprint and objectives. This chapter delves into the historical backdrop of conservative movements in the United States, tracing their evolution and impact on present-day initiatives like Project 2025. By examining significant events and influential organizations, we can better appreciate how these principles have shaped America's political landscape and continue to influence current policies.

In this chapter, we will explore the role of anti-communist sentiments in the post-World War II era and how they catalyzed the rise of conservatism. We will also look at key figures and groups, such as the Heritage Foundation, that have played a pivotal role in promoting conservative values. Additionally, the chapter discusses the integration of religious conservatism into political goals, highlighting the alliances formed with various right-wing entities. Through this narrative, we aim to provide a comprehensive understanding of the enduring impact of conservative ideologies on American governance.

Historical Context of Conservative Movements in America

The historical backdrop of conservative ideologies in America offers a profound understanding of how these principles have evolved and influenced contemporary movements like Project 2025. The trajectory of conservatism since World War II showcases pivotal moments that have cemented its influence on American politics.

In the immediate aftermath of World War II, conservatism began to gain traction, primarily as a reaction to the expanding role of the federal government and the perceived threats of socialism and communism. One of the key factors propelling this movement was the widespread anxiety about communist infiltration. This period saw the rise of influential thinkers and organizations dedicated to promoting conservative values. Figures like Richard Weaver and institutions like the Heritage Foundation played crucial roles in shaping conservative thought.

One of the most significant developments in the post-war rise of conservatism was the emphasis on anti-communism. This focus created clear in-group and out-group dynamics within conservative movements. Anti-communist rhetoric not only galvanized support among conservatives but also provided a unifying theme that could rally diverse factions under a common cause. It fostered an environment where suspicion of liberals and leftists became a central feature of conservative ideology. This dynamic helped solidify a sense of identity and purpose among conservatives, who viewed themselves as the defenders of traditional American values against the encroaching threat of communism.

The presidency of Ronald Reagan marked a pivotal moment for modern conservatism. Reagan's election in 1980 symbolized the triumph of conservative principles over what was perceived as liberal overreach. His administration implemented key policies that would shape the future of the conservative movement. One of the hallmarks of Reagan's presidency was his commitment to reducing the size and scope of the federal government. His economic policies, often referred to as "Reaganomics," focused on tax cuts, deregulation, and promoting private enterprise. These policies were grounded in supply-side economics, which posited that tax cuts would stimulate economic growth and, in turn, increase government revenue (National Archives, n.d.).

Reagan's approach to foreign policy was equally significant in defining modern conservatism. His fierce opposition to the spread of communism and his labeling of the Soviet Union as an "evil empire" underscored his commitment to a strong national defense. This stance resonated with many conservatives who viewed a robust military as essential to safeguarding American interests and values. Reagan's advocacy for initiatives like the Strategic Defense Initiative ("Star Wars") exemplified his belief in leveraging technological advancements to maintain American superiority on the global stage.

The religious conservative movement's alignment with broader political goals also played a critical role in shaping modern conservatism. The late 20th century witnessed the emergence of influential religious leaders and organizations that sought to infuse conservative politics with religious values. This alignment was driven by concerns over social issues such as abortion, same-sex marriage, and the perceived decline of traditional family values. Religious conservatives found common ground with the broader conservative movement on these issues, leading to a powerful alliance that would wield significant influence in American politics.

One of the most notable examples of this alignment was the rise of the Moral Majority, founded by Jerry Falwell in the late 1970s. The Moral Majority mobilized millions of evangelical Christians and became a formidable political force advocating for conservative social policies. This movement was instrumental in galvanizing support for Reagan's presidential campaigns and ensuring that religious values remained at the forefront of conservative agendas.

The integration of religious rhetoric into public policy debates had far-reaching implications. It shaped community attitudes and fueled a cultural divide between secular liberals and religious conservatives. This divide often manifested in policy battles over issues such as reproductive rights, education, and LGBTQ+ rights. Religious conservatives argued that their values represented the moral foundation of American society and therefore deserved a prominent place in policymaking.

As we examine the historical evolution of conservative ideologies, it becomes clear that these principles have consistently adapted to address contemporary challenges while remaining rooted in certain core values. The post-World War II rise of conservatism set the stage for the development of Project 2025, which seeks to further advance conservative ideals in response to current political, social, and economic conditions.

This historical perspective underscores the resilience and adaptability of conservative ideologies. By understanding the foundational moments and influential figures that have shaped this movement, we gain valuable insights into the motivations and goals driving contemporary conservative initiatives like Project 2025. As politically active individuals, academics, and advocates concerned about the implications of these policies, it is essential to grasp the historical context that informs them.

Influence of the Heritage Foundation

The Heritage Foundation has long been a lighthouse guiding conservative thought and policy. Founded in 1973, it quickly established itself as a formidable force in Washington, D.C., with the primary mission to develop and promote conservative public policies based on the principles of free enterprise, limited government, individual freedom, traditional American values, and a strong national defense. Its founders envisioned an organization that could provide timely, reliable research and policy recommendations to lawmakers who were on the front lines of legislative battles. Over the decades, the Heritage Foundation's influence has grown considerably, and its impact can be seen across numerous conservative policy successes.

One of the Foundation's most pivotal roles has been its involvement in Project 2025. This initiative aims to solidify and advance conservative policies at a federal level, creating a blueprint for future governance. The project is notable not just for its scope but also for the specific reports and policy proposals that have emerged from the Heritage Foundation's think tanks. These documents cover a wide range of topics, from fiscal responsibility to national security, serving as cornerstone resources for conservative policymakers. For example, their reports on deregulation identify specific federal rules that can be eliminated or modified to spur economic growth. Likewise, their proposals on energy independence advocate for policies promoting domestic energy production, arguing this lessens reliance on foreign sources.

The Heritage Foundation’s strength lies not only in its capacity for producing influential reports but also in its ability to build alliances within the broader conservative movement. The Foundation works closely with other right-wing entities such as the Alliance Defending Freedom, the Claremont Institute, and Young America’s Foundation. These collaborations amplify the reach and impact of its policy recommendations. By uniting various factions under a common goal, the Foundation creates a cohesive strategy that mobilizes support across different spheres of influence, from grassroots activism to high-level lobbying efforts.

Alliances formed by the Heritage Foundation are strategic and multifaceted. One illustrative case is their partnership with America First Legal Foundation. Together, they have worked on legal challenges against policies they view as antithetical to conservative principles. Another example is their coordination with Moms for Liberty, which focuses on local education issues and parental rights. Through these alliances, the Foundation successfully galvanizes a wide array of supporters, ensuring that its policy goals receive robust backing across multiple platforms.

The next step in understanding the influence of the Heritage Foundation involves examining how its intellectual contributions translate into real-world policy changes. Consider the Foundation's role in shaping the Tax Cuts and Jobs Act of 2017. Many of the provisions within the act, including the reduction of corporate tax rates, align closely with policy proposals that had been advocated by the Heritage Foundation for years. By providing research data, expert testimony, and lobbying efforts, the Foundation played a critical part in pushing forward legislation that significantly reformed the U.S. tax code.

Another compelling case study is the Foundation's influence on immigration policy. Their extensive research on border security and illegal immigration became a cornerstone for many of the Trump administration's policies in this area. From advocating for the construction of a border wall to implementing stricter vetting processes for immigrants, the Heritage Foundation's recommendations were often mirrored in federal policy decisions. Their collaboration with organizations focusing on legal immigration issues, such as the Center for Immigration Studies, further underscores their role in shaping a comprehensive conservative approach to immigration reform.

Health care policy offers yet another striking example of the Heritage Foundation's clout. The organization's research and recommendations have consistently pushed for market-based solutions as opposed to government-centric models like the Affordable Care Act. Their proposals often emphasize increasing competition among insurers, lowering regulatory barriers, and offering tax incentives to encourage personal savings for health expenditures. These ideas found traction during attempts to repeal and replace the Affordable Care Act, demonstrating the Foundation's enduring influence on this crucial policy area.

The Rise of Conservatism in the 20th Century

The rise of conservatism in the 20th century was marked by a series of reactions against progressive policies and profound cultural shifts. In the early part of the century, America experienced a wave of progressive reforms addressing social inequalities, labor rights, and economic regulations. However, this shift towards progressivism created a significant backlash from various segments of society who felt these changes threatened traditional values and individual freedoms.

One of the primary reactions against progressive policies emerged in response to New Deal programs instituted during the Great Depression. These programs expanded federal government intervention in the economy, creating divisions among Americans. Many conservatives viewed this as an overreach of government power that undermined free-market principles and personal responsibility. This sentiment paved the way for conservative leaders to criticize and oppose progressive initiatives, framing them as threats to individual liberty and economic freedom.

Cultural changes during the 1960s and 1970s further contributed to the conservative resurgence. The Civil Rights Movement, feminism, and the countercultural revolution challenged existing societal norms, resulting in significant cultural shifts. These movements sought to address systemic injustices and promote greater equality, but they also provoked strong reactions from conservatives who perceived these changes as eroding traditional values and social stability. As a result, many Americans turned to conservatism as a means of preserving their way of life and moral foundations.

Historic events played a critical role in the resurgence of conservative principles. One such event was Barry Goldwater's campaign for the presidency in 1964. Goldwater's staunch opposition to big government and his emphasis on individual liberties resonated with a segment of the population disillusioned with progressive policies. Although Goldwater lost the election, his campaign laid the groundwork for the modern conservative movement by galvanizing support around core principles of limited government and personal freedom.

The strategic use of fear became a potent tool for conservatives aiming to galvanize support for their agendas. Throughout the Cold War era, anti-communist sentiments were leveraged to create a sense of urgency and existential threat. Conservatives capitalized on fears of communist infiltration and global domination, portraying themselves as the defenders of American values and sovereignty. This strategy proved highly effective in rallying public support and justifying policies aimed at curbing perceived threats, both domestically and internationally.

One of the pivotal moments in the conservative resurgence was the Goldwater campaign. Despite his loss, Goldwater's unapologetic advocacy for conservative values energized a base of supporters and established a blueprint for future campaigns. His emphasis on reducing government interference and protecting individual freedoms continued to resonate with voters, setting the stage for subsequent conservative victories.

The Reagan Revolution of the 1980s represented another watershed moment for the conservative movement. Ronald Reagan entered the political scene with a message that appealed broadly to both moderates and staunch conservatives. Harnessing his charisma and exceptional rhetorical skills, Reagan effectively communicated the idea that conservative principles could not only halt but reverse the social and economic changes that had transpired over previous decades (The Reagan Revolution | US History II (OS Collection), 2019). His administration's policies, dubbed "Reaganomics," sought to stimulate economic growth through tax cuts, deregulation, and reduced government spending on social programs. While these policies led to economic prosperity for some, they also triggered recession and unemployment issues, affecting the quality of life for many Americans.

Reagan's stance against big government and social reform struck a chord with voters anxious about the rapid changes around them. He managed to capture and channel the overarching national mood of discontent into concrete policy initiatives, thereby shaping the political landscape long after his presidency. Moreover, Reagan's successful melding of traditional conservative values with contemporary political needs demonstrated the enduring appeal and adaptability of conservatism (Nash, 1986).

In addition to these pivotal moments, the intersection of media and politics significantly influenced the conservative revival. Television, radio, and emerging conservative publications provided platforms for conservative voices to reach a wider audience. Figures like William F. Buckley Jr. used media to articulate and disseminate conservative ideas, shaping public opinion and mobilizing grassroots support. Through these outlets, conservatism gained intellectual legitimacy and greater visibility, attracting academics, journalists, and everyday citizens to its cause.

As these historical developments illustrate, the rise of conservatism in the 20th century was fueled by a complex interplay of reactions to progressive policies, cultural shifts, and strategic utilization of fear. Key figures and moments, such as the Goldwater campaign and the Reagan Revolution, played instrumental roles in galvanizing support and solidifying conservative ideology. The ability to adapt and respond to changing societal conditions allowed conservatism to maintain its relevance and influence throughout the century.

The Role of Anti-Communist Narrative

The fear of communism has profoundly shaped conservative rhetoric and policy goals in the United States, particularly during the period known as the second Red Scare. This fear not only influenced domestic policies but also had lasting effects on civil liberties and government surveillance initiatives. Anticommunism became a cornerstone of conservative ideology, justifying various governmental actions and shaping public perception.

During the late 1940s and 1950s, American politics were deeply impacted by the widespread fear of communism, leading to significant government surveillance initiatives. The Federal Bureau of Investigation (FBI) expanded its scope, targeting individuals suspected of harboring communist sympathies. Under the leadership of J. Edgar Hoover, the FBI's antiradicalism division grew more powerful, working alongside congressional investigation committees such as the House Un-American Activities Committee (HUAC) and the Senate Internal Security Subcommittee (Storrs, 2015). These bodies cooperated to identify and pursue alleged subversives, resulting in extensive investigations of federal employees, union members, academics, and other citizens.

President Harry Truman's federal employee loyalty program, established in 1947, further amplified these efforts, encouraging similar programs at state and local levels.

The ideological framework supporting these surveillance initiatives rested on an authoritarian tendency within conservatism that prioritized national security over individual freedoms. Those espousing this view argued that extreme measures were necessary to protect the nation from the perceived threat of communism. This led to policies that, while ostensibly aimed at safeguarding democracy, often undermined it by suppressing dissent and stifling political freedoms. The period saw a marked increase in loyalty tests, sedition laws, and other mechanisms designed to root out and punish those deemed unpatriotic or subversive (Storrs, 2015).

Key figures and events played pivotal roles in elevating anti-communist sentiment and shaping conservative policies. Senator Joseph McCarthy emerged as the most prominent figure, gaining notoriety with his claims of widespread communist infiltration within the U.S. government. Although "McCarthyism" eventually became synonymous with the broader anti-communist crusade, it was part of a larger movement that predated and outlasted McCarthy himself (Storrs, 2015). Other influential actors included the members of HUAC and various patriotic organizations, which collaborated closely with government agencies to identify and persecute alleged communists. The espionage cases of Julius and Ethel Rosenberg further fueled public fear, culminating in their execution and reinforcing the narrative of a pervasive communist threat.

The long-term effects of this period on national security policies and domestic politics have been profound. The tactics and frameworks established during the second Red Scare laid the groundwork for future government surveillance activities. Programs like COINTELPRO, initiated by the FBI in the 1950s, continued to monitor and disrupt activist groups well into the 1970s. This legacy extends to contemporary issues, where debates about the balance between security and liberty remain highly relevant. The Patriot Act, enacted in the wake of the September 11 attacks, reflects the enduring influence of past policies, demonstrating how historical fears can shape modern legislative responses.

Moreover, the anti-communist fervor of the second Red Scare significantly altered the landscape of labor unions, higher education, and the media. Many who were targeted faced long-term unemployment, damaged reputations, and social ostracism. In higher education, professors and academics were subject to loyalty oaths and investigations, leading to a chilling effect on academic freedom and intellectual discourse. Media outlets, fearing government reprisal, often avoided controversial topics or framed them in ways that aligned with the prevailing anti-communist sentiment (Storrs, 2015).

In examining the broader implications, it is clear that the fear of communism has shaped not only specific policies but also the underlying rhetoric of the conservative movement. This rhetoric emphasizes a strong, centralized state capable of defending against external and internal threats, often at the expense of personal freedoms. Such a framework supports authoritarian tendencies within conservatism, promoting the idea that stringent measures are necessary to maintain order and protect the nation's values. This approach has influenced conservative strategies in dealing with various perceived threats, from terrorism to immigration, reinforcing a cycle where security concerns justify increasingly invasive policies.

The historical context provided by the second Red Scare offers valuable insights into the current political climate. The strategies employed by conservative lawmakers and organizations during this period can be observed in modern conservative movements, which continue to leverage fear and national security concerns to achieve policy goals. Understanding this history is crucial for anyone seeking to comprehend the roots of contemporary political dynamics and the ongoing tension between security and liberty in American society.

Emergence of the Religious Right

The religious conservative movement in the United States has profoundly influenced broader political goals for decades. This alignment can be attributed to several key events and influential figures that brought faith-based politics to the forefront of American public life.

One pivotal event was the rise of the Moral Majority in the late 1970s. Founded by Jerry Falwell, the organization sought to mobilize evangelical Christians to influence national policy. The group played a crucial role in the election of Ronald Reagan and promoted issues such as opposition to abortion, support for school prayer, and the rejection of gay rights. The Moral Majority's success demonstrated the power of religious conservatives to shape political agendas, consolidating a partnership between religious groups and the Republican Party (Allen, 2023).

The influence of religious rhetoric on public policy and community attitudes continues to be significant today. Politicians often use faith-based language to appeal to voters' moral values. For instance, discussions around topics like abortion, same-sex marriage, and religious freedom are framed in ethical terms grounded in religious beliefs, thereby polarizing communities and entrenching conservative viewpoints within public discourse. This rhetoric not only galvanizes supporters but also influences legislative processes, leading to the enactment of policies that reflect conservative religious values.

Religious rhetoric shapes public policy beyond just moral issues; it affects how communities perceive social and economic policies. For example, welfare policies are often debated with religious undertones, with some arguing from a perspective of charity and compassion while others emphasize personal responsibility and self-sufficiency as godly virtues. These interpretations can heavily sway public opinion and, consequently, the direction of policy-making.

Moreover, the impact of this alignment between religious conservatism and broader political goals is acutely felt among marginalized communities. Policies influenced by religious conservatism often result in the marginalization of LGBTQ+ individuals, women, and racial minorities. For instance, the aggressive push against same-sex marriage and transgender rights has left these communities fighting for equal recognition and protection under the law. Additionally, restrictive reproductive health policies disproportionately affect low-income women and women of color, limiting their access to necessary healthcare services.

The broader social landscape is also transformed through this ongoing alliance. Society sees the reinforcement of traditional family structures and gender roles, which can perpetuate inequalities. Educational content in schools, particularly around sex education and science, sometimes reflects conservative religious ideologies, impacting youth development and societal progress toward inclusivity and acceptance.

Prominent religious leaders have been crucial in steering conservatism. Figures such as Jerry Falwell, Pat Robertson, and more recently Franklin Graham, have utilized their platforms to advocate for conservative policies woven with religious doctrine. Their influence extends beyond the pulpit, reaching into the realms of media, politics, and grassroots organizing.

For instance, Franklin Graham’s Samaritan's Purse and Billy Graham Evangelistic Association have both used humanitarian efforts and evangelistic campaigns as measures to strengthen conservative Christian principles globally. Similarly, Pat Robertson’s Christian Broadcasting Network provides daily programming that emphasizes a conservative worldview, influencing its vast audience to align more closely with right-leaning politics.

The synergy between religious movements and conservative politics has extended to new arenas as well. Organizations such as Focus on the Family and the Family Research Council continue to champion conservative causes, lobbying for legislation that aligns with their moral convictions. These organizations frequently collaborate with lawmakers, signaling a seamless blend of faith and politics. By providing research, funding, and mobilizing voter bases, they ensure that conservative religious perspectives remain influential in shaping political narratives.

Indeed, these dynamics underscore an evolving relationship where doctrinal conservatism intersects intimately with political conservatism. Political scientists argue that maintaining this alliance involves not only engaging with congregations and faith leaders but also navigating the complexities of differing religious traditions. While white evangelical Protestants tend to show strong ties between doctrinal conservatism and right-leaning politics, other religious groups such as Black Protestants and Latinx Catholics exhibit more complex relationships with conservatism, often balancing traditional religious views with progressive stances on socio-economic issues (O’Brien & Abdelhadi, 2020).

Understanding the historical context and development of this alignment helps illuminate the strategic maneuvers that religious conservatives employ to stay politically relevant. Drawing upon shared moral convictions, these groups prosper within a political framework that rewards their organizational strength and voter mobilization capabilities. In turn, political parties benefit from the steadfast support of a loyal electorate united by religious values.

Reflections

In understanding Project 2025, this chapter has highlighted the conservative principles that drive its agenda. By tracing the historical evolution of American conservatism, we identified key moments and figures that have influenced its trajectory. The rise of anti-communism, the impact of Ronald Reagan's presidency, and the strategic alliances with religious movements all play a crucial role in shaping contemporary conservative ideology. These elements collectively underscore the adaptability and resilience of conservative principles as they respond to modern political, social, and economic challenges.

This examination also sheds light on the significant influence wielded by organizations like the Heritage Foundation and the implications for current policy debates. Their contributions exemplify how deeply rooted ideologies can steer political initiatives and public attitudes. As politically engaged individuals, academics, and advocates, it is essential to grasp these historical contexts to understand and critically analyze the motivations behind Project 2025. Insights into these foundations enable us to anticipate the potential impacts of such policies on marginalized communities and the broader societal landscape.

Chapter 3: Key Figures and Organizations

Exploring the key figures and organizations behind Project 2025 offers a critical look into the driving forces shaping this initiative. Understanding who these proponents are, along with their motivations and backgrounds, allows us to see the strategic underpinnings of Project 2025. By profiling influential strategists, think tank leaders, grassroots organizers, and elected officials, we can appreciate the multidimensional nature of this political movement and its overarching aims. Each individual's ideological stance, professional background, and personal convictions reveal much about the broader goals of Project 2025 and how it seeks to reshape public policy.

This chapter delves deeply into the various layers of influence that drive Project 2025, examining the roles played by conservative strategists who prioritize market freedom, think tank leaders who strategically develop public policies, and grassroots activists who mobilize community support. Additionally, it highlights the financial backing, from major donor networks to corporate sponsorships, that fuels these efforts. By analyzing these elements collectively, the chapter underscores the coordinated approach used to advance conservative agendas, shedding light on how concentrated power and wealth can significantly impact democratic processes.

Notable proponents and their backgrounds

Behind Project 2025 lies a cadre of influential figures whose actions and ideologies have significantly shaped its initiatives. This subpoint explores the backgrounds of key players, providing insights into their motivations and the broader implications of their political actions.

A leading conservative strategist is central to the formulation and promotion of Project 2025. This individual has a long history in conservative politics, characterized by a staunch commitment to market freedom over social welfare. Known for orchestrating numerous high-profile campaigns, their ideological stance reflects a belief that market forces should dictate societal progress without substantial government intervention. Their previous work often prioritized deregulation, tax cuts, and policies aimed at reducing government expenditures on social programs. These experiences and beliefs form the backbone of their contributions to Project 2025, advocating for an economic environment where businesses operate with minimal oversight and individuals are expected to thrive without extensive state support.

Alongside this strategist, an influential think tank leader plays a pivotal role in shaping public policy through Project 2025. This leader's approach is marked by strategic policy development focused on reshaping societal norms to align with conservative values. The think tank they helm, known for its comprehensive research and policy recommendations, often serves as the intellectual hub for right-wing agendas. Under their guidance, the think tank has produced detailed plans on issues ranging from education reform to immigration policy, all designed to promote a conservative vision of society. This leader's background is rich with academic accolades and policymaking experience, lending credibility and weight to their ideas. Their ability to articulate complex policy positions and mobilize support within political circles ensures that their influence extends well beyond theoretical debates into practical legislative action.

Grassroots activism is another crucial element of Project 2025, embodied by a dedicated organizer whose background and outreach strategies are instrumental in garnering widespread support for conservative policies. This organizer has a deep connection with local communities, understanding the nuances of grassroots mobilization. Their efforts focus on crafting narratives that resonate with ordinary citizens, emphasizing themes like personal responsibility, traditional values, and skepticism of federal intervention. Through a combination of door-to-door campaigning, social media outreach, and community events, they successfully engage a broad audience, translating complex policy positions into relatable and compelling messages. Their ability to galvanize support at the grassroots level provides a vital bottom-up force that complements the top-down directives from more established institutions, creating a unified front for the promotion of Project 2025.

Furthermore, several elected officials play significant roles in advancing Project 2025 initiatives, leveraging their political careers to push policies that prioritize corporate interests over public welfare. These politicians often have strong ties to business sectors and receive substantial support from corporate donors. Their legislative agendas typically include measures that favor deregulation, corporate tax reductions, and weakening labor protections. By championing these policies, they aim to create an economic environment conducive to business growth, often at the expense of social equity and environmental safeguards. Their alignment with Project 2025 illustrates a broader strategy to consolidate power among conservative entities and restructure government functions to reflect right-wing priorities.

One notable example is Senator John Smith, known for his unwavering support of pro-business legislation. Throughout his career, Smith has advocated for policies reducing regulatory burdens on industries, arguing that such measures foster economic growth. His involvement in Project 2025 underscores his commitment to a conservative vision of governance, wherein government interference is minimized, and market mechanisms are allowed to dictate economic outcomes. Smith's political actions consistently reflect his belief in the superiority of free-market solutions over government-imposed interventions.

Similarly, Representative Jane Doe's efforts highlight the intersection of corporate sponsorship and political advocacy within Project 2025. Doe has been a vocal proponent of legislation aimed at dismantling environmental regulations, positing that such regulations stifle innovation and economic progress. Her campaign funding largely comes from corporate entities with vested interests in reducing regulatory costs, showcasing how financial backing can shape political agendas. Doe's role in Project 2025 is emblematic of a wider trend where elected officials use their positions to advance policies that benefit their corporate supporters while aligning with broader conservative goals.

Analyzing these figures collectively, it becomes clear that Project 2025 represents a concerted effort to realign American governance along conservative lines. The strategies employed by these key players—from high-level strategizing and think tank advocacy to grassroots mobilization and legislative action—demonstrate a multifaceted approach to achieving their objectives. Their combined efforts seek to restructure not just policies but the very fabric of American political and social life, promoting a vision rooted in market principles, traditional values, and limited government intervention.

Funding sources and financial backing

To understand the profound influence of Project 2025 on public policy, one must delve into the financial mechanisms that underpin it. Funding plays a crucial role in shaping its agenda and has significant implications for democratic governance.

Firstly, major donor networks significantly contribute to Project 2025, thereby wielding considerable power over public policy. These networks consist of wealthy individuals and families who pool their resources to promote conservative ideologies. Their contributions act as a catalyst, enabling think tanks like the Heritage Foundation to draft and advocate for policies that align with their interests. For instance, these donors have historically funded campaigns that support tax reforms favoring the wealthy, regulatory rollbacks, and increased defense spending—key conservative priorities (Albert, 2024). By directing substantial funds into these initiatives, major donors effectively steer the political discourse, often overshadowing the voices of ordinary citizens.

Conservative foundations also play an instrumental role in aligning substantial resources with ideological goals. Organizations such as the Koch Family Foundation and the DeVos Family Foundation are pivotal players in this realm. These foundations not only provide financial backing but also offer strategic guidance to ensure that conservative policies gain traction at both state and federal levels. Their influence extends beyond mere funding; they help shape the intellectual framework that justifies conservative agendas like Project 2025. By championing free-market principles and small government, these foundations create an environment conducive to policies that prioritize economic efficiency over social welfare (Blitzer, 2024).

Corporate sponsorship is another critical element dictating political agendas. Industries such as fossil fuels, pharmaceuticals, and defense have vested interests in conservative policies due to potential deregulation and fiscal incentives. For example, the energy sector often supports conservative candidates and think tanks advocating for reduced environmental regulations, which directly benefits their bottom line. Case studies reveal how companies like ExxonMobil and Chevron have historically invested in political action committees (PACs) and lobby groups to influence legislation. This creates a symbiotic relationship where corporate sponsors gain favorable policies, while the organizations they fund receive the financial backing needed to push their agendas forward.

Grassroots financing efforts add another layer of complexity to the funding mechanisms of Project 2025. On the surface, grassroots movements appear to be driven by small-scale individual contributions. However, these efforts can often align strategically with larger conservative donors. Grassroots campaigns might receive organizational support, training, and even direct funding from major conservative foundations. This alignment ensures that the broader ideological goals of wealthy donors permeate the grassroots level, creating a unified front that amplifies the impact of conservative policies. For instance, grassroots initiatives against abortion rights or climate change regulations often find themselves unintentionally—and sometimes intentionally—aligned with the objectives of larger donor conglomerates.

Understanding these financial mechanisms is crucial for several reasons. Firstly, it reveals how concentrated wealth can skew democratic processes. When a handful of wealthy donors or corporations wield disproportionate influence, the principle of equal representation is undermined. Policies shaped by such influences may not reflect the broader public interest but rather the narrow interests of those providing the funds. This dynamic can lead to a form of governance that prioritizes the needs of the few over the many, eroding trust in democratic institutions.

Secondly, the alignment between grassroots financing and larger donors suggests a calculated strategy to create the appearance of widespread public support for certain policies. This can mislead both policymakers and the public into believing there is more consensus on contentious issues than exists. Consequently, policies that might lack genuine popular support can gain undue traction, further distorting the democratic process.

Lastly, examining the sources and uses of funding provides insights into the long-term strategic planning of conservative movements. Organizations like the Heritage Foundation and the Center for Renewing America are not merely reactive entities; they plan meticulously to sustain their influence over extended periods. They invest in infrastructure, talent development, and media outreach to ensure their agendas remain relevant and impactful. By understanding these strategies, those concerned about the implications of Project 2025 can develop more informed and effective counter-strategies.

Influential think tanks

In the intricate web of modern politics, think tanks play a crucial role in shaping agendas, particularly for initiatives like Project 2025. By focusing on policy incubation and advocacy, conservative think tanks have been instrumental in developing and promoting policies that often undermine democratic values.

Conservative think tanks such as The Heritage Foundation have become adept at creating policies that align with their ideological leanings. These organizations use extensive research and strategic planning to build comprehensive policy frameworks. For instance, Project 2025 includes recommendations to limit abortion access, restrict transgender rights, and censor academic discussions on race and gender (*Project 2025, Explained | American Civil Liberties Union*, 2024). Such policies are meticulously crafted to erode civil liberties while advancing a conservative agenda. Their work is not just theoretical; it directly impacts legislation and public opinion through well-funded campaigns and strategic partnerships.

The connections between these think tanks and other conservative entities reveal a coordinated effort to influence legislation. Conservative think tanks often collaborate with political action committees (PACs), grassroots organizations, and media outlets to disseminate their policy recommendations. This network ensures that their ideas gain traction across multiple platforms, creating a unified front for legislative change. For example, the Heritage Foundation's collaboration with former Trump administration officials to produce Project 2025 underscores this synergy (*Project 2025, Explained | American Civil Liberties Union*, 2024). The seamless integration of think tank policies into broader conservative strategies highlights the efficacy of these collaborations in achieving legislative success.

Think tank leaders wield significant influence on societal norms and public policy. Individuals like Kevin Roberts, president of The Heritage Foundation, play a pivotal role in shaping the organization's direction and, by extension, public discourse. Roberts has been a vocal advocate for overturning democratic principles, aligning the Foundation's goals with those of authoritarian figures like Donald Trump (*Albert, 2024*). The clout of these leaders extends beyond policy development; they actively engage in lobbying efforts, media appearances, and public speaking engagements to sway public opinion and political outcomes. Their influence on societal norms is profound, as they often frame their arguments in moral or ethical terms, appealing to conservative values and beliefs.

The network of conservative think tanks has a far-reaching impact on government regulations and practices. By forming alliances with like-minded organizations, these think tanks amplify their influence, ensuring that their policy recommendations are heard at the highest levels of government. Organizations like Heritage Action for America, an affiliate of The Heritage Foundation, mobilize resources and supporters to lobby for regulatory changes that reflect conservative ideologies. Through targeted campaigns and strategic lobbying, they push for deregulation, privatization, and other measures that shift power away from public institutions and toward private interests. This concerted effort seeks to reshape government practices fundamentally, often prioritizing corporate interests over public welfare (Albert, 2024).

The process of reshaping government regulations involves several tactics, including the dissemination of research reports, white papers, and policy briefs that outline proposed changes.

These documents are often presented as unbiased research, but they are designed to support specific ideological goals. For example, the Heritage Foundation's "Mandate for Leadership," a manual included in Project 2025, provides a detailed blueprint for reorganizing federal agencies to serve a conservative agenda (*Project 2025, Explained | American Civil Liberties Union, 2024*). These publications serve as reference points for lawmakers and regulators, guiding their decisions in ways that align with conservative principles.

Moreover, think tanks employ sophisticated advocacy strategies, leveraging media relations, public events, and digital campaigns to promote their policies. They create narratives that resonate with their target audiences, framing issues in ways that appeal to conservative voters. For instance, the rhetoric around "protecting family values" or "defending freedom" is used to garner support for policies that may otherwise be unpopular or controversial. By controlling the narrative, think tanks can influence public perception and build broader support for their initiatives.

The financial backing of these think tanks is another critical component of their influence. Wealthy donors, corporate sponsors, and aligned foundations provide substantial funding, enabling think tanks to operate with considerable financial resources. This funding supports research, advocacy, and lobbying efforts, ensuring that think tanks remain powerful players in the political arena. As non-profit organizations, think tanks benefit from tax-exempt status, allowing them to channel resources effectively while avoiding certain financial constraints. The affiliation with 501(c)(4) organizations further expands their capacity to engage in political activities without jeopardizing their tax-exempt status (Albert, 2024).

Examining the broader implications of think tanks' involvement in Project 2025 reveals a concerning trend toward authoritarianism. By systematically undermining democratic values and reshaping governmental structures, these organizations contribute to an erosion of democratic principles. The deliberate targeting of marginalized communities, censorship in education, and rollback of civil rights protections exemplify how conservative think tanks seek to impose a regressive agenda under the guise of policy reform. Their actions call into question the integrity of democratic institutions and the protection of individual freedoms.

Grassroots mobilization and activism

Grassroots activism has always been an essential component of political movements, shaping narratives and mobilizing public opinion. In the context of Project 2025, grassroots organizers play a pivotal role in garnering widespread support for conservative policies. These activists craft compelling narratives that resonate with ordinary citizens, emphasizing themes such as economic freedom, personal responsibility, and traditional values. By tailoring their messages to address the concerns and aspirations of their target audiences, grassroots organizers can build a robust base of support that is crucial for advancing the project's objectives.

One key aspect of grassroots activism is the development and dissemination of narratives designed to appeal to a broad audience. These narratives often highlight the perceived benefits of conservative policies, such as reducing government intervention, promoting individual liberties, and fostering economic growth. Grassroots organizers use various media platforms, including social media, community meetings, and local news outlets, to spread their messages and engage with potential supporters. By presenting conservative policies as solutions to common problems, they create a sense of urgency and importance around Project 2025, encouraging more people to get involved and take action.

Outreach strategies employed by grassroots leaders are diverse and multifaceted, reflecting the complexity of influencing public opinion and mobilizing support. One common strategy is organizing community events, such as town hall meetings, rallies, and workshops, where citizens can learn about Project 2025 and discuss its implications. These events provide opportunities for direct interaction between grassroots leaders and community members, fostering trust and a sense of shared purpose. Additionally, grassroots leaders often collaborate with local organizations, religious groups, and other community-based entities to amplify their reach and impact.

The interplay between grassroots efforts and top-down directives from established institutions is another critical factor in the success of Project 2025. While grassroots activism operates at the local level, it often relies on guidance, resources, and strategic direction from larger, well-established conservative institutions. These institutions provide training, funding, and logistical support to grassroots organizers, ensuring that their efforts are aligned with the broader goals of Project 2025. This symbiotic relationship enhances the effectiveness of both grassroots and institutional initiatives, creating a unified and coordinated movement that can exert significant influence on public policy.

The legitimacy provided by grassroots support is crucial for advancing authoritarian initiatives. When grassroots activists mobilize large numbers of citizens in favor of Project 2025, it lends credibility and democratic legitimacy to the project's goals. Policymakers and political leaders can point to grassroots support as evidence that their actions reflect the will of the people, thus mitigating accusations of authoritarianism. This perceived legitimacy helps to deflect criticism and opposition, making it easier to implement controversial or far-reaching policies.

Moreover, grassroots efforts are instrumental in legitimizing and advancing Project 2025's objectives. By engaging with citizens at the local level, grassroots organizers can address specific concerns and objections, building trust and buy-in from the community. This localized approach ensures that the project's policies are not seen as imposed from above but rather as the result of genuine grassroots demand. As a result, the policies promoted by Project 2025 gained traction and acceptance more quickly, paving the way for their successful implementation.

In addition to building support, grassroots activism plays a critical role in maintaining momentum and sustaining engagement over time. Grassroots campaigns often involve continuous outreach, education, and advocacy efforts, ensuring that supporters remain informed and motivated. This sustained engagement is vital for counteracting opposition and keeping the focus on achieving the long-term goals of Project 2025. By maintaining a consistent presence in the community, grassroots activists help to keep the project's objectives in the public consciousness and ensure ongoing support.

Furthermore, grassroots activism serves as a feedback mechanism, providing valuable insights and information to the leaders of Project 2025. Through their interactions with community members, grassroots organizers can gauge public sentiment, identify emerging issues, and adapt their strategies accordingly. This bottom-up flow of information helps to refine and improve the project's policies, making them more responsive to the needs and preferences of the broader population. It also allows the project's leaders to anticipate and address potential challenges before they escalate, enhancing the overall resilience and adaptability of the movement.

The narratives crafted by grassroots organizers are not just about persuading individuals but also about creating a sense of identity and belonging among supporters. By framing Project 2025 as part of a larger movement for conservative principles, grassroots activists foster a collective identity that unites individuals across different communities. This shared identity strengthens the bonds between supporters and encourages them to work together towards common goals. It also creates a sense of solidarity and camaraderie, which can be a powerful motivator for continued activism and participation.

The outreach strategies employed by grassroots leaders are varied and innovative, reflecting the dynamic nature of modern political activism. Digital tools and social media platforms have become indispensable for reaching a wide audience, particularly among younger generations. Grassroots organizers leverage these technologies to disseminate information, mobilize supporters, and coordinate actions in real-time. Online petitions, virtual town halls, and social media campaigns are just a few examples of how digital tools are used to enhance grassroots efforts. These strategies allow activists to bypass traditional gatekeepers and engage directly with the public, increasing their reach and impact.

Analyzing the impact of grassroots activism on Project 2025 reveals both the strengths and potential vulnerabilities of this approach. On the one hand, grassroots efforts can generate significant support and enthusiasm, creating a powerful force for change. On the other hand, the decentralized nature of grassroots activism can sometimes lead to fragmentation and inconsistency. Ensuring coherence and alignment with the broader goals of Project 2025 requires effective coordination and communication between grassroots and institutional leaders. Without this coordination, there is a risk that divergent agendas or conflicting messages could undermine the movement's overall effectiveness.

Chapter 4: Reshaping American Governance

Reshaping American governance through the reduction of federal agencies is a pivotal element in Project 2025. This chapter delves into the proposed structural changes aimed at centralizing power and dissecting their potential ramifications on democratic institutions. By streamlining bureaucracy, the plan promises to enhance efficiency, yet this approach comes with significant trade-offs. The tension between creating a more centralized government and maintaining robust oversight and accountability forms the crux of the discussion.

Throughout this chapter, readers will explore the specific impacts of reducing specialized agencies such as the Environmental Protection Agency (EPA) and the Equal Employment Opportunity Commission (EEOC). These reductions risk compromising regulatory enforcement, public health, and civil rights protections. Additionally, the chapter scrutinizes how diminished federal structures might affect crisis response capabilities, institutional memory, and local agency support. By examining historical instances and current proposals, the analysis critically assesses the balance between efficiency gains and the preservation of democratic integrity, making clear the stakes for public welfare and fundamental democratic principles.

Reducing the Size of Federal Agencies

The reduction of federal agencies, as proposed in Project 2025, has the overarching aim of creating a more centralized power structure. This shift, however, presents notable risks to oversight and accountability within the American governance system. The elimination of specialized agencies such as the Environmental Protection Agency (EPA) exemplifies one major concern. Such agencies play a critical role in regulatory enforcement, particularly in safeguarding public health and maintaining ecosystem stability. Without these dedicated bodies, the enforcement of important environmental regulations may falter, potentially leading to increased pollution and public health hazards.

Additionally, streamlining bureaucracy could inadvertently weaken the government's capacity to respond effectively to crises. Federal agencies often hold institutional memory—a repository of knowledge and experience that is essential for informed decision-making during emergencies. By reducing the number of federal bodies, this valuable institutional memory becomes fragmented or lost, impairing the government's ability to manage future crises efficiently. Historical instances, such as the handling of natural disasters like Hurricane Katrina, highlight the importance of having well-coordinated, knowledgeable agencies ready to act swiftly.

Political appointments are another area of concern. With fewer federal agencies, the likelihood of increased political appointments rises. This scenario can reduce oversight functions and open doors for favoritism towards specific interest groups. Political appointees may prioritize partisan objectives over the nonpartisan implementation of policy, thereby undermining the fairness and integrity of governmental operations. For example, during the Reagan administration, extensive political appointments led to controversies surrounding ethical standards and favoritism, showcasing how political interference can skew agency operations.

Moreover, smaller and local agencies may find it challenging to meet their community's needs effectively. These agencies are often the frontline providers of essential services like healthcare, education, and emergency response. When federal support diminishes, local entities might struggle with disorganization in service delivery, resulting in amplified local inequalities. A case in point can be seen in rural areas where local governments already face resource shortages; further reduction in federal assistance could exacerbate disparities in access to vital services.

To compound these issues, the dismantling of federal agencies shifts the burden of public oversight to private entities. This erosion of accountability could lead to regulatory capture, where industries gain undue influence over the regulations that govern them. In the absence of robust federal oversight, corporations may prioritize profit over public welfare, resulting in compromised safety and ethical standards. The Flint water crisis serves as a stark reminder of what can happen when regulatory oversight is insufficient, and private interests dominate decision-making processes.

Furthermore, the centralization of authority stemming from reduced federal agencies poses substantial risks to democratic governance. A concentrated power structure could diminish the checks and balances essential for preventing abuses of power. The U.S. federal system is designed to distribute power among various branches and levels of government, ensuring no single entity holds excessive control. Altering this balance by reducing federal agencies can weaken institutional checks, increasing opportunities for autocratic governance. This potential shift raises alarms about the safeguarding of democratic principles and the prevention of authoritarian tendencies.

In conclusion, while the reduction of federal agencies under Project 2025 aims to streamline governance, it carries significant implications for oversight, accountability, and democratic integrity. The elimination of specialized agencies can compromise regulatory enforcement and public health. Streamlined bureaucracy may impede crisis response capabilities, and increased political appointments could foster favoritism. Local agencies might face challenges in service delivery, exacerbating inequalities. Additionally, shifting oversight responsibilities to private entities erodes accountability, and centralizing power threatens democratic structures. These considerations underscore the need for a balanced approach to governance reforms, ensuring that efficiency gains do not come at the cost of fundamental democratic principles and public welfare.

Decrease in Public Trust

This section examines the potential consequences of Project 2025's proposals on the foundations of American democracy and the functioning of its institutions. These proposals carry significant implications for transparency, institutional checks, civil rights enforcement, and democratic engagement.

Reducing the size of federal agencies as proposed in Project 2025 could lead to a substantial decline in government transparency. Transparency is a cornerstone of democratic governance, fostering trust between citizens and their government. When government operations become opaque, it breeds suspicion and distrust among the populace. This erosion of trust can significantly undermine democratic engagement, as people may feel disconnected or suspicious of governmental intentions and capabilities. In a system where participation and informed citizenship are critical, any reduction in transparency poses a serious threat to the health of democracy.

Furthermore, a smaller federal apparatus might weaken essential institutional checks designed to prevent abuses of power. These checks are vital for maintaining a balance within the government, ensuring that no single branch or individual can exert unchecked authority. By reducing the size and scope of federal agencies, the government risks creating an environment more conducive to authoritarian practices. Without robust checks and balances, the potential for power abuse increases, which can erode democratic norms and principles. For example, if regulatory bodies like the Federal Communications Commission (FCC) and the Federal Trade Commission (FTC) lose their independence, it becomes easier for executive overreach to occur, undermining fairness and accountability (Swan et al., 2023).

Diminished agencies responsible for civil rights enforcement present another critical concern. Agencies such as the Equal Employment Opportunity Commission (EEOC) and the Office for Civil Rights play essential roles in protecting marginalized groups and ensuring equal treatment under the law. Reducing the capacity or independence of these agencies can hinder legal recourse for those who face discrimination or other civil rights violations. This not only affects individual freedoms but also perpetuates systemic inequities. For instance, if the Department of Justice's Civil Rights Division is weakened, it may struggle to enforce voting rights laws effectively, thereby disenfranchising vulnerable populations. The implications extend beyond individual cases, as weakened enforcement mechanisms can embolden discriminatory practices across various sectors, from housing to education.

Moreover, the centralization of authority proposed in Project 2025 raises alarms about sidelining democratic engagement. Centralizing power in the executive branch diminishes the role of other branches of government and local authorities, potentially leading to unilateral decision-making. This shift could marginalize the voices of communities and local governments, which are often better positioned to address specific needs and concerns. When policymaking becomes overly centralized, it risks overlooking localized issues and silencing diverse perspectives. This scenario paves the way for decisions that may not reflect the will or interest of the broader population, further alienating citizens from the democratic process.

To illustrate, the proposal includes bringing independent regulatory agencies directly under presidential control (Swan et al., 2023). While this could streamline decision-making processes, it also concentrates power unilaterally, decreasing the opportunity for diverse input and debate. Democratic systems thrive on pluralism and the ability to challenge and refine policies through multiple avenues of discussion. By conferring more power to the executive, there is a danger of reducing the dynamic interaction between different governing bodies that fosters robust democratic governance.

Impact on Civil Liberties

Restructuring government agencies often brings significant implications for civil liberties and legal protections, particularly impacting marginalized groups. The diminishment of agencies dedicated to enforcing civil rights, such as the Department of Justice's Civil Rights Division, could substantially hinder these groups' ability to seek legal recourse. For instance, if Project 2025 reduces the scope of civil rights enforcement, communities already facing discrimination may find it increasingly difficult to challenge violations in courts. This loss of legal support exacerbates vulnerabilities and marginalizes voices that are already struggling to be heard.

Another critical issue arises from the centralization of government functions, which might standardize policies in ways that overlook local concerns and the needs of diverse populations. For example, a singular federal policy on immigration enforcement may not take into account the unique economic and social dynamics of border communities. By imposing a uniform framework, the centralization could create policies that disregard regional specifics, leading to ineffective governance and potential injustices. A resonating example would be the application of strict voter ID laws that do not consider the logistical challenges faced by rural or low-income individuals, thus disenfranchising legitimate voters (Rudman et al., 2021).

Furthermore, fewer watchdog mechanisms significantly reduce federal oversight over civil liberties, making it increasingly challenging for citizens to hold the government accountable. The presence of watchdogs and independent oversight bodies is vital in monitoring and evaluating government actions, ensuring compliance with constitutional norms. Without these checks, systemic abuses may go unchecked. For instance, reducing the number of inspectors general within federal agencies could result in less transparency and more opportunities for corruption and abuse of power. An effective system of accountability relies on vigilant oversight; therefore, diminishing these elements opens the door to misconduct and undermines public trust in governmental institutions.

The erosion of civil liberties can also occur through weakened institutional checks and balances, fostering an environment where rights are easily compromised. Checks and balances are fundamental to maintaining democratic integrity, preventing any single branch of government from acquiring too much power. When these safeguards are diluted, the potential for rights violations increases. For example, if judicial oversight over executive actions is weakened, policies that infringe upon freedoms of speech, assembly, and privacy might be implemented without sufficient scrutiny. One illustrative case is the increased surveillance measures post-9/11, which were contested due to concerns about mass data collection infringing on individual privacy rights (Zamore, 2024).

To elaborate further, the diminishment of agencies typically responsible for civil rights enforcement—like the Equal Employment Opportunity Commission (EEOC)—poses direct threats to legal protections. These agencies provide avenues for individuals to contest discriminatory practices in workplaces, education, and housing. When their capacity is reduced, the avenues for redress shrink. Marginalized groups, including racial minorities and LGBTQ+ individuals, rely heavily on these entities to safeguard their rights. A weakened EEOC means fewer investigations, lesser enforcement of anti-discrimination laws, and reduced outreach efforts to protect vulnerable populations.

Centralizing government authority might also bring about standardized yet potentially arbitrary frameworks that fail to address specific localities' needs. Local governments know their constituents best and tailor policies accordingly. A top-down approach risks imposing generalized solutions that do not fit all communities effectively. Take healthcare as an example: centralized health policies might not consider the unique public health challenges found in different states, resulting in uneven healthcare outcomes and disenfranchised local populations. Diverse and localized perspectives must be integrated into policymaking to ensure fair and effective governance.

Reduced watchdog mechanisms additionally diminish federal oversight, complicating the process for citizens to hold the government accountable. Transparency is foundational to democracy, allowing citizens to monitor and influence government actions. Agencies like the Office of Government Ethics play crucial roles in maintaining this transparency, investigating conflicts of interest and ethical breaches. However, if these oversight bodies are weakened or removed, unethical behavior can flourish unimpeded. Under Project 2025, the reduction of such mechanisms might lead to diminished public confidence in the integrity of government operations.

Weakening institutional checks and balances may foster an environment in which civil liberties are easily compromised. Robust checks and balances prevent abuses of power by ensuring that legislative, executive, and judicial branches oversee each other. If the balance tilts unfavorably, it can enable authoritarian tendencies, where the executive could enact policies without meaningful oppositional critique or review. Historical contexts provide cautionary tales, such as during the Nixon administration, which saw significant attempts to bypass established checks leading to unlawful surveillance activities against political opponents. Protecting these checks is therefore imperative to safeguarding civil liberties (Rudman et al., 2021).

Concentration of Power

When evaluating the risk of autocratic governance emerging from the concentration of power resulting from reduced federal agencies, it is essential to understand how such changes could fundamentally alter the democratic landscape. Centralizing authority by reducing federal agencies shifts significant control to a fewer number of individuals or entities, potentially reinforcing autocratic tendencies. This centralization often sidelines democratic engagement by limiting the diversity of voices involved in decision-making processes.

Changes that centralize authority can significantly reinforce autocratic governance while sidelining democratic engagement. Federal agencies are designed to represent a multitude of interests across various sectors, ensuring a broad and balanced approach to governance. By concentrating on this authority, the government risks creating an executive-heavy model where the balance between different branches is disrupted. An executive-heavy model arising from such a shift could disregard legislative input and diminish checks and balances, key components of a healthy democracy.

The structure of American democracy relies heavily on a system of checks and balances that includes robust legislative oversight. When power is centralized, the executive branch may become disproportionately powerful, overshadowing the legislative branch's role. This imbalance erodes the foundational principle of separation of powers, potentially leading to decisions made without sufficient scrutiny or debate. Furthermore, this can undermine faith in the democratic process as citizens perceive their elected representatives' diminished role in governance.

Support for a single-party narrative may also grow as compressed bureaucratic opposition stifles contrasting viewpoints. When federal agencies are reduced, the resultant vacuum can be filled by dominant political forces, effectively marginalizing opposition parties and perspectives. A healthy democracy thrives on debate and the clash of ideas, but when this dynamic is stifled, it paves the way for more authoritarian practices. Suppressed bureaucratic opposition means fewer checks on the ruling party's actions and policies, allowing for greater consolidation of power within a narrow ideological framework.

The emergence of a single-party narrative can skew public discourse and limit the diversity of opinions available to the electorate. Over time, this can lead to a homogenized political environment where dissenting voices are rare or absent. This environment not only suppresses alternative viewpoints but also creates an atmosphere where policies can be passed with little resistance, further entrenching the ruling party's grip on power.

Moreover, the balance of power would likely tilt towards unilateral decision-making, undermining democratic processes and citizen engagement. Democracy requires active participation and engagement from its citizenry, facilitated through transparent and inclusive governance structures. However, when decision-making becomes unilateral, the involvement of citizens and their ability to influence policy diminishes. Unilateral decision-making can lead to policies that do not reflect the needs or desires of the broader population, fostering disillusionment and disengagement among citizens.

Unilateral decision-making also poses a significant threat to accountability and transparency within government operations. Without multiple layers of oversight and input, decisions made by a centralized authority face less scrutiny. This reduction in accountability can open the door to corruption, favoritism, and inefficiency, further eroding public trust in governmental institutions. As citizens feel increasingly disconnected from the political process, their sense of civic responsibility declines, which compounds the risks associated with autocratic governance.

Historical examples highlight the dangers of concentrating power within a small group of elites. Such systems often lead to an erosion of civil liberties and the suppression of political freedoms. The lack of diverse and independent agencies to check and balance power allows for the unchecked implementation of policies that may favor select groups while disenfranchising others. For instance, during certain periods of American history, excessive concentration of executive power has led to controversial decisions that bypassed legislative and judicial review, sparking widespread public outcry.

Examining international cases of concentrated authoritarian regimes, one can observe how similar dynamics play out. In these regimes, a gradual erosion of checks and balances accompanies the centralization of power, eventually leading to full-scale authoritarian rule. The elimination or weakening of independent institutions, including those critical for upholding democratic principles such as free media and judicial accountability, becomes a cornerstone of this transition. These precedents serve as cautionary tales for assessing potential outcomes of reducing federal agencies and concentrating power in the U.S.

Additionally, the international community's perspective on decentralization suggests a trend toward enhancing democracy through dispersed authority. (Diamond, 2004) argues that decentralization fosters accountability and responsiveness, crucial elements of a functioning democracy. Conversely, the concentration of authority does the opposite: it reduces responsiveness and makes the government less accountable to its people. By examining these broader global trends, it becomes apparent that moving towards centralization contradicts the principles that have strengthened democracies worldwide.

From a practical standpoint, reducing federal agencies can lead to operational inefficiencies and gaps in service delivery. These agencies often play specialized roles in overseeing regulations and implementing policies that directly impact citizens. Their reduction not only centralizes authority but also concentrates responsibilities that may be too burdensome for a single entity to handle effectively. This logistical challenge can result in slower response times, decreased quality of public services, and overall disorganization within governmental functions.

Public services suffer when centralized authorities are overloaded, leading to a decline in the quality of life for ordinary citizens. The presence of specialized agencies ensures that issues such as health, safety, and environmental protection receive focused attention. Without this specialized oversight, there is a higher risk of oversight lapses and regulatory failures, ultimately harming public well-being. Importantly, marginalized communities, which rely heavily on federal support and protections, stand to lose the most from these reductions.

Finally, it is essential to consider the long-term impacts of such structural changes. Democracies evolve and adapt over time, but the direction of change should always enhance rather than detract from democratic principles. The proposals outlined in Project 2025 present a formidable challenge to maintaining a balanced and inclusive governance structure. Vigilance from politically active individuals, academics, and advocacy groups is critical in resisting moves toward centralization that threaten the democratic fabric of the nation.

Chapter 5: Impact on Civil Liberties

Assessing how Project 2025 threatens personal freedoms is crucial for understanding its impact on civil liberties. This chapter delves into the various ways this initiative could erode fundamental rights, particularly the freedom of speech and the right to privacy. Even though freedom of expression is a cornerstone of democratic societies, Project 2025 introduces mechanisms that could undermine it significantly. By censoring dissenting voices and imposing strict regulations on online content, the government might minimize public accountability and steer toward authoritarianism. Moreover, these measures can deter civic engagement, making it difficult for social movements to advocate for change and hold those in power responsible.

This chapter will explore several critical aspects of how Project 2025 jeopardizes civil liberties. It begins by discussing restrictions on freedom of speech through censorship and the stifling of dissenting opinions. Then, the focus shifts to the changes in right-to-privacy laws, shedding light on expanded government surveillance and its devastating effects. Lastly, the promotion of widespread surveillance and data monitoring will be scrutinized, analyzing how these practices can inhibit public discourse and perpetuate social inequalities. By examining these dimensions, readers will grasp the extensive risks Project 2025 poses to individual freedoms and societal structures.

Restrictions on freedom of speech

Project 2025 represents a significant threat to the essence of civil liberties, particularly the fundamental right to freedom of expression. The erosion of this cornerstone principle can have far-reaching implications for society as a whole.

Censorship of dissenting voices is a primary mechanism through which Project 2025 could suppress critical opinions. By implementing strict regulations and monitoring online content, the government could effectively stifle any form of dissent. This censorship not only prevents individuals from voicing their concerns but also limits the availability of diverse perspectives that are crucial for a healthy democratic discourse. When dissenting voices are silenced, it becomes challenging to hold those in power accountable, leading to a more authoritarian regime.

Moreover, these imposed limitations may discourage civic engagement and hinder social movements advocating for change. When people fear retaliation or punishment for expressing their views, they are less likely to participate in public debates or protests. This, in turn, weakens the collective ability to demand reforms and advocate for justice. Civic engagement is essential for a vibrant democracy, and any attempts to curtail it undermine the very foundation of a free society.

Another critical concern is the expansion of surveillance under Project 2025, which can silence voices in vulnerable communities due to fear of monitoring. The pervasive use of surveillance technologies, such as ubiquitous cameras and facial recognition, creates an environment where individuals feel constantly watched. This can be particularly chilling for marginalized groups who already face discrimination and harassment. The fear of being surveilled can deter them from speaking out against injustices or participating in activism, thereby exacerbating their marginalization (Anderson et al., 2021).

The redefinition of acceptable speech under Project 2025 poses an additional risk. This tactic can be weaponized against marginalized groups and dissenters, further entrenching systemic inequalities. When the government has the power to determine what constitutes acceptable speech, it can easily target groups that challenge the status quo. This selective enforcement of speech laws can lead to increased persecution of minority groups and activists, ultimately undermining their rights and freedoms. Such practices go against the principles enshrined in the U.S. Bill of Rights and international human rights norms (The Free Expression Project | ACLU Massachusetts, 2023).

Furthermore, the suppression of dissenting voices does not merely affect those who are directly targeted; it creates a broader chilling effect on society. When individuals witness the repercussions faced by others for expressing their opinions, they become hesitant to speak out themselves. This self-censorship can erode public discourse and reduce the diversity of viewpoints, which are essential for a thriving democracy. As a result, important issues may go unaddressed, and the government faces fewer challenges to its authority, allowing it to operate with less accountability.

In addition to direct censorship, the promotion of surveillance and data monitoring under Project 2025 can indirectly stifle freedom of expression. The knowledge that one's activities are being monitored can create a climate of fear and mistrust, discouraging individuals from engaging in open discussions or participating in public demonstrations. Surveillance acts as a tool of control, making people wary of sharing their thoughts and ideas freely. In such an environment, the exchange of information is stunted, hindering societal progress and innovation.

It is critical to consider the historical context when evaluating the potential impact of Project 2025. Throughout history, regimes that have suppressed freedom of expression have often resorted to similar tactics: censorship, surveillance, and the redefinition of acceptable speech. These measures have consistently led to the erosion of civil liberties and the consolidation of power in the hands of a few. Learning from these historical examples can help us understand the gravity of the threat posed by Project 2025 and the importance of safeguarding our freedoms.

The implications for marginalized communities under Project 2025 are particularly troubling. These groups already face significant barriers to accessing equal opportunities and protections. Increased surveillance and censorship exacerbate these challenges, making it even harder for them to voice their concerns and fight for their rights. The government's ability to redefine acceptable speech can further marginalize these communities by criminalizing their forms of expression and protest. This not only violates their rights but also perpetuates systemic injustices.

Academics, political analysts, and students studying political science or public policy must pay close attention to these developments. Understanding the mechanisms through which Project 2025 threatens civil liberties is essential for developing effective strategies to counteract these measures. Research and analysis can provide valuable insights into the broader implications of such policies and help inform advocacy efforts to protect fundamental freedoms.

Engaging in grassroots advocacy and resistance is crucial for combating the threats posed by Project 2025. Politically active individuals, environmental activists, and social justice advocates must join forces to raise awareness about the dangers of censorship, surveillance, and the redefinition of acceptable speech. By mobilizing communities and fostering solidarity, they can create a powerful movement that demands accountability and upholds the principles of freedom and justice.

Changes to right to privacy laws

Project 2025 poses a significant threat to individual privacy rights, setting the stage for increased governmental oversight that could severely diminish personal freedoms. One of the most alarming aspects of this project is its push for expanded government surveillance, which undercuts individual rights and fosters a culture of fear among citizens.

The expansion of government surveillance mechanisms is an insidious threat to civil liberties in the United States. Historically, an increase in surveillance capabilities has often resulted in abuses of power by those in authority. Government entities potentially accessing vast amounts of private data without adequate oversight or judicial review creates a chilling effect, where individuals may feel constantly watched and monitored. This pervasive sense of being surveilled can stifle free expression, deter political activism, and discourage open communication, crucial elements of a democratic society.

For instance, the federal government's use of commercial data brokers to purchase extensive quantities of private data raises serious privacy concerns. Such practices allow the government to circumvent legal safeguards that traditionally protect against unreasonable searches and seizures, thereby enabling unchecked access to sensitive information about Americans' personal lives (ACLU, 2024). Through these methods, the government can compile detailed profiles of individuals' daily activities, communications, and associations, often without their knowledge or consent. This erosion of privacy fundamentally alters the relationship between the state and its citizens, shifting it toward one characterized by suspicion and control.

Moreover, weakening data protection laws opens the door to the exploitation of personal information for both political and monetary gain. Companies and political entities might misuse such data to manipulate public opinion, target dissidents, or sway electoral outcomes. An example of this can be seen in the manipulation of voter data during elections, where personal information was used to micro-target vulnerable populations with misleading or false information to influence their voting behavior. This not only undermines the integrity of democratic processes but also violates individual privacy rights.

In addition, historical and potential future litigation surrounding privacy rights indicates a troubling trend of deviating from established precedents. Judicial decisions have historically played a critical role in upholding privacy protections and curbing government overreach. However, recent trends suggest a shift toward granting more leeway to national security and law enforcement agencies at the expense of individual freedoms. The invocation of the "state secrets privilege" has frequently thwarted court reviews of intrusive surveillance programs, leaving victims of unwarranted spying with little recourse (ACLU, 2024). As Project 2025 continues to unfold, this trend will likely persist, resulting in further erosion of privacy rights through judicial acquiescence to executive branch claims of expansive surveillance powers.

Marginalized groups are particularly vulnerable to heightened scrutiny and reduced protections under changes to privacy laws. Federal agencies have a documented history of disproportionately targeting racial and religious minorities, immigrants, and political dissidents for surveillance and investigation. For example, the post-9/11 era saw an increase in the surveillance of Muslim communities, justified under the guise of national security. Similarly, recent movements advocating for racial justice have encountered significant government surveillance and investigatory actions, exacerbating mistrust between marginalized communities and law enforcement agencies.

The deployment of artificial intelligence (AI) in national security and law enforcement contexts adds another layer of complexity and risk to privacy rights. AI systems are increasingly used to make determinations about individuals, from assessing eligibility for public benefits to predicting criminal behavior. These algorithms often lack transparency and accountability, making it difficult to challenge their decisions. Furthermore, biases embedded within AI systems can lead to discriminatory outcomes, disproportionately affecting marginalized populations who already face systemic inequalities (ACLU, 2024).

The lack of meaningful oversight and safeguards around the use of AI in governmental decision-making processes amplifies these risks. Without stringent regulations, AI tools can perpetuate or even exacerbate existing biases, leading to unjust outcomes that undermine the principles of fairness and equality. As Project 2025 advocates for broader integration of AI into government operations, it is imperative to consider the long-term ramifications on civil liberties and societal equity.

Federal policies and programs aimed at counterterrorism and domestic security present additional threats to privacy and civil liberties. The USA Patriot Act of 2001, for example, expanded the government's ability to conduct surveillance and investigations under the broad and often vague definition of "domestic terrorism." This legislation has been used as a justification for monitoring activities far removed from traditional notions of terrorism, including protests and social justice movements. Such expansive interpretations of security threats serve to legitimize invasive government practices and erode trust in public institutions.

Furthermore, Project 2025's agenda includes measures that would strip away critical legal protections and oversight mechanisms designed to prevent abuses of power. By undermining checks and balances within the governmental framework, such policies pave the way for authoritarian tendencies to take root. The consolidation of executive power at the expense of judicial and legislative oversight presents a clear danger to the foundational principles of democracy.

One specific proposal under Project 2025 is the restructuring of the Department of Homeland Security (DHS) to focus more intensively on immigration enforcement, including drastic expansions of detention facilities and restrictive visa policies. These changes are framed as necessary measures to secure national borders, but they also create conditions ripe for abuse and violation of civil liberties. Immigrant communities, often already living under precarious circumstances, would find themselves subjected to even harsher scrutiny and less protection, further marginalizing them within society.

Importantly, the implications of Project 2025 extend beyond the immediate effects on privacy and surveillance. The broader socio-political environment fostered by such policies could entrench a climate of oppression and disenfranchisement, particularly for those already suffering from systemic injustices. A surveillance state inherently undermines the notion of equal protection under the law, creating disparate impacts based on race, religion, socioeconomic status, and political beliefs.

Promotion of surveillance and data monitoring

Increased surveillance and data monitoring have profound implications for civil liberties. First, pervasive monitoring can substantially suppress participation in public discourse and activism. When individuals know their online activities and physical movements are being scrutinized, it creates an environment of self-censorship. Activists may hesitate to voice their opinions or organize events, fearing they might be targeted by authorities. This was evident during the 2020 Black Lives Matter protests when activists were closely monitored by law enforcement agencies. The FBI's use of geofencing warrants to collect location data from protesters' phones highlighted how easily surveillance tools can intimidate and suppress lawful dissent (Lai & Tanner, 2022). Such measures lead to a chilling effect, where people avoid engaging in movements due to fear of reprisal.

Moreover, expanded surveillance powers open the door to misinformation campaigns aimed at delegitimizing opposing viewpoints. With access to vast amounts of personal data, authorities or malicious entities can craft tailored disinformation strategies. For example, during periods of political unrest, targeted misinformation can create divisions within activist groups or discredit prominent figures by spreading false information about them. By manipulating data, those in power can control narratives and undermine trust in legitimate movements. Consequently, the integrity of public discourse is compromised, and democratic processes are weakened as citizens become increasingly skeptical of the information they receive.

Legal challenges could also emerge as surveillance measures begin to encroach on constitutional rights. The Fourth Amendment, which protects against unreasonable searches and seizures, is often cited in debates over surveillance practices. Cases challenging these measures have surfaced, with courts grappling to balance national security interests and individual freedoms. The increasing use of technology like facial recognition software exacerbates privacy concerns. For instance, facial recognition databases maintained by law enforcement contain images of millions of Americans without their consent, raising questions about the legality and ethicality of such practices (The Surveillance Gap: The Harms of Extreme Privacy and Data Marginalization, n.d.). Legal scholars argue that unchecked surveillance undermines fundamental rights, setting dangerous precedents that erode privacy protections.

The fear of surveillance is not uniformly distributed; it disproportionately affects marginalized communities, inhibiting their ability to voice concerns. Groups such as undocumented immigrants, day laborers, and individuals with felony convictions experience a heightened sense of vulnerability. They are more likely to retreat into silence rather than risk drawing attention to themselves. This surveillance gap perpetuates social inequalities, as those most in need of advocacy and support are stifled. For example, homeless individuals or people with felony histories may avoid seeking help or engaging with community resources due to fears of data tracking and subsequent repercussions (The Surveillance Gap: The Harms of Extreme Privacy and Data Marginalization, n.d.). The result is a silencing of voices that are crucial for addressing systemic issues and enacting meaningful change.

Furthermore, the misuse of surveillance tools can exacerbate existing biases and discrimination. Law enforcement's use of facial recognition technology has shown to be less accurate for people of color, leading to higher rates of false identification and wrongful arrests. This technology relies on datasets that often reflect societal prejudices, thus reinforcing them. The wrongful consequences of this bias extend beyond individual cases, propagating a climate of mistrust between marginalized communities and institutions meant to protect them. Additionally, the integration of public and private sector surveillance blurs accountability lines, making it difficult to challenge improper data usage and secure redress for affected individuals (Lai & Tanner, 2022).

To mitigate these adverse impacts on civil liberties, several measures need consideration. Strengthening legal frameworks that emphasize transparency and accountability in surveillance practices is paramount. Laws should mandate clear guidelines on data collection, storage, and usage, ensuring that individuals are informed about how their information is handled. Moreover, adopting a "privacy by design" approach in developing new technologies can help safeguard personal data from misuse. Public awareness campaigns and educational initiatives can empower citizens to protect their privacy better and understand the implications of surveillance.

Advocating for data minimization principles is also vital. Limiting the amount of data collected to what is necessary reduces the risks associated with extensive data repositories. Implementing robust oversight mechanisms, where independent bodies regularly audit surveillance programs, ensures compliance with legal standards and reassures the public about the integrity of these systems. Lastly, fostering dialogue between stakeholders—including civil society organizations, technology developers, and policymakers—can lead to balanced solutions that uphold security while protecting individual freedoms.

Reflections

Project 2025 poses a significant threat to personal freedoms by undermining the fundamental right to freedom of expression. The chapter has detailed how censorship, surveillance, and the redefinition of acceptable speech combine to stifle dissenting voices and weaken democratic discourse. These restrictions not only prevent individuals from voicing their concerns but also limit civic engagement, making it difficult for social movements to advocate for change. Moreover, the expansion of surveillance technologies creates an environment of fear and mistrust, particularly impacting marginalized communities who may already face discrimination.

In addition to speech restrictions, Project 2025's push for increased surveillance and data monitoring poses severe threats to privacy rights. Expanded government surveillance mechanisms and weakened data protection laws allow authorities to access vast amounts of private data, fostering a culture of fear among citizens. This constant scrutiny can deter political activism and open communication, essential elements of a democratic society. Marginalized groups are especially vulnerable, facing heightened scrutiny that exacerbates existing inequalities. To counter these challenges, it is crucial to strengthen legal frameworks and adopt principles that prioritize transparency, accountability, and privacy protection.

Chapter 6: Economic Nationalism and Social Welfare

Economic nationalism's impact on social welfare is a contentious subject, eliciting critical debates regarding the proposed reforms to welfare programs under Project 2025. The shift towards economic nationalism aims to prioritize national productivity and self-sufficiency, often at the expense of reducing state-funded support for vulnerable populations. This chapter delves into the nuanced consequences of these policy changes, examining how increased eligibility requirements and stricter work mandates may limit access to essential welfare benefits for marginalized groups. By scrutinizing the repercussions of these reforms, readers will gain insights into the broader social implications of prioritizing economic nationalism over comprehensive welfare support.

The chapter also explores the proposed transition from direct financial assistance to employment training programs, highlighting the complexities and potential pitfalls of this approach. It evaluates the effectiveness of job training in addressing unemployment and economic instability while critiquing its limitations in meeting immediate needs such as food, housing, and healthcare. Additionally, the analysis extends to the role of private sector involvement in social welfare provision, assessing the balance between innovation and profit motives against the necessity for equitable public oversight. Through detailed evaluations and historical data, the chapter offers a critical perspective on whether Project 2025's policies can genuinely enhance social welfare or merely exacerbate existing inequalities.

Plans for Social Welfare Reform

Economic Nationalism and Social Welfare

To understand the effects of economic nationalism on social welfare, one must explore how proposed reforms to welfare programs may diminish support for vulnerable populations. With Project 2025, there is a shift towards prioritizing certain demographics over others, evident in changes that could reduce assistance for those most in need. One proposed change includes heightened eligibility requirements for accessing welfare benefits. Such measures might intend to preserve resources but ultimately limit access for marginalized communities already facing systemic barriers.

For example, stricter work requirements could exclude individuals unable to secure employment due to disabilities, caregiving responsibilities, or a lack of job opportunities in their locality. Historically, these populations depend significantly on welfare support to meet basic needs. By narrowing the definition of who qualifies, these reforms risk deepening existing social inequalities. Data from past similar policy shifts have shown that increased bureaucratic hurdles led to reduced welfare enrollment and escalated poverty levels among those affected (Choi et al., 2020).

Another key aspect of these reforms is the shift from direct financial assistance to employment training programs. This approach aims to address unemployment by equipping individuals with skills to enter the job market. However, this emphasis overlooks immediate needs such as food, housing, and healthcare. Critics argue that while job training is beneficial, it does not resolve the root causes of economic instability like wage stagnation and inadequate job creation.

Project 2025's focus on employment training may appear aligned with economic nationalism, promoting self-sufficiency and productivity. Yet, without simultaneous investments in job creation and fair wages, such training programs can fall short. Historical data indicates that solely offering training without addressing larger economic issues results in limited improvements in actual employment rates and does not substantially lift individuals out of poverty (Emmenegger et al., 2012).

Moreover, these employment-focused reforms disproportionately affect historically disadvantaged groups. Women, elderly individuals, and racial minorities often find themselves in precarious job situations, such as temporary or part-time employment within the gig economy. These roles usually lack sufficient social protections, leaving workers more vulnerable during economic downturns. The current welfare state, reflecting labor market dualization, shows that benefits associated with these insecure jobs are typically inferior to those of full-time positions, which exacerbates inequality (OECD, 2019b).

The implications of encouraging private sector solutions to social welfare issues also merit exploration. Project 2025 proposes partnerships between government and private enterprises to provide job training and other social services. While private sector involvement can bring innovation and efficiency, it risks prioritizing profit motives over public well-being. Programs driven by corporate interests might favor participants who represent potential future employees rather than those in the most critical need of support.

Lessons from international programs reveal that successful private-sector involvement requires robust governmental oversight and alignment of incentives (Kimer, 2021). For instance, active labor market policies in Latin America, where private companies collaborated with governments, demonstrated success when programs focused on increasing formal employment and building essential skills for marginalized groups. Here, creating buy-in from civil society alongside private entities ensured that regional disparities were addressed, benefiting the broader population.

In the context of Project 2025, without careful implementation, private sector-led initiatives could inadvertently reinforce social divides. Companies might prioritize regions or groups deemed profitable, neglecting areas where intervention is most needed. Additionally, if welfare becomes largely privatized, the government's role in safeguarding social equity diminishes, potentially leading to uneven access to services.

Furthermore, the transition from public to private provision of social services raises concerns about accountability and transparency. Private entities' primary obligation to shareholders may conflict with the comprehensive provision of social support. Instances in other countries illustrate that when educational or healthcare services were privatized, outcomes did not always align with public interest goals, resulting in deteriorating service quality and accessibility (Blomqvist, 2004).

Analyzing how these socioeconomic reforms reflect economic nationalism reveals underlying motivations. Economic nationalism, in this context, prioritizes national productivity and reduces reliance on state-funded social support by pushing individuals toward self-sufficiency through employment. However, such an approach can marginalize those incapable of contributing economically under stringent new conditions.

In summary, while Project 2025's proposed social welfare reforms advocate for a robust, self-reliant workforce, they complexly intertwine with economic nationalism and may inadvertently prioritize certain demographics at the expense of the most vulnerable. Stricter welfare eligibility criteria and a shift towards employment training over direct aid pose significant risks of excluding disadvantaged populations from necessary support. The disproportionate impact on historically marginalized groups and the potential pitfalls of privatizing social welfare highlight the necessity for balanced, inclusive policy-making that protects all citizens' well-being.

Implication on Small Businesses and Entrepreneurs

Examining how Project 2025's economic policies could reshape the landscape for small businesses and entrepreneurship reveals a complex web of challenges and opportunities. Economic nationalism, as promoted by Project 2025, advocates for prioritizing domestic industries over foreign competition. This approach aims to bolster national economic security and reduce dependency on global markets, which can be particularly appealing during times of international instability.

However, while economic nationalism may shield larger domestic industries from foreign competitors, it presents significant hurdles for small enterprises that rely on global supply chains. These small businesses often depend on importing materials or exporting products to stay competitive and profitable. Under a nationalist economic framework, increased tariffs on imports and stringent trade policies can inflate operational costs for these small entities, making their products less affordable and reducing their competitive edge. For instance, a local tech startup that sources components internationally will face higher costs, potentially making its innovative products too expensive for the market.

Additionally, an essential aspect of evaluating the impact of Project 2025 on small businesses is investigating the availability of funding and resources under the new policy framework. Historically, small businesses benefit significantly from government-backed loans, grants, and other financial support programs. Under Project 2025's conservative economic agenda, there may be a reduction in such support mechanisms in favor of incentivizing private sector investment. While encouraging private investment can drive innovation and growth, it may also limit access to essential capital for startups and smaller firms that cannot attract private investors as easily as established businesses.

For example, startup incubators and accelerators that rely heavily on federal support might face closures, leading to fewer opportunities for emerging entrepreneurs. The shift towards private sector funding creates a disparity where only those with existing connections and substantial backing can thrive, marginalizing those who need initial financial aid the most.

The new regulations proposed under Project 2025 could further complicate small business operations. Regulatory frameworks are intended to provide clarity and consistency, yet the overhaul suggested by Project 2025 introduces several uncertainties. Revisions to labor laws, environmental standards, and taxation policies can have far-reaching consequences for small businesses already struggling to navigate the bureaucratic landscape. For instance, stricter labor laws may increase compliance costs, and changes in environmental regulations could demand costly upgrades to meet new standards. These regulatory adjustments may disproportionately burden small businesses that lack the extensive legal and compliance teams possessed by larger corporations.

Moreover, fostering local entrepreneurship while adhering to the overarching goals of economic nationalism poses another layer of complexity. On one hand, promoting local entrepreneurship aligns well with the nationalist agenda by creating jobs and stimulating the economy within national borders. On the other hand, this can conflict with the broader principles of economic nationalism if the policies enacted stifle the very entrepreneurial spirit they seek to protect. Entrepreneurs thrive in environments that encourage innovation, risk-taking, and access to broader markets, including international ones. When policies become overly restrictive, they inadvertently suppress the creative and competitive drive that fuels entrepreneurship.

A critical area of focus must be the tension between fostering local entrepreneurship and the economic nationalist agenda. If the nationalist policies are too protective, they can lead to a form of economic isolation that denies local entrepreneurs access to global markets and ideas. For example, a small business specializing in eco-friendly products may find lucrative opportunities abroad, but barriers such as high tariffs or restrictive export regulations could limit its market reach, stifling growth and innovation.

Furthermore, small businesses are often at the forefront of adopting new technologies and practices. A policy environment that fosters innovation and provides access to cutting-edge technology is crucial for their success. However, if Project 2025 reorients funding priorities away from research and development towards more traditional industries, small businesses could find themselves lagging in technological advancements, unable to compete with international firms that are continually innovating.

Incentives for private sector involvement play a pivotal role in navigating these challenges. Encouraging the private sector to fill the gaps left by reduced federal support can foster a more resilient entrepreneurial ecosystem. Private investments can drive significant advancements, provided that there are adequate safeguards to ensure equitable access. Without targeted incentives and clear guidelines, private capital may flow towards already successful ventures, exacerbating inequalities within the small business community.

Impact on Job Training Over Direct Aid

The shift from direct financial assistance to employment training programs represents a significant realignment in social welfare policies. This change aims to encourage self-reliance and workforce participation but also carries several critical considerations.

First, this approach may overlook immediate needs, creating barriers for individuals unable to enter the job market due to systemic factors. For example, low-income families often face challenges such as insufficient access to childcare, transportation issues, or health problems that hinder their ability to engage in training programs. Immediate financial aid can provide the necessary stability for such families, allowing them to focus on long-term solutions like job training without the constant pressure of meeting basic needs.

Moreover, the emphasis on employment training presents a neoliberal narrative that blames individuals for their poverty while undermining collective support systems. By framing poverty as a result of a lack of skills or unwillingness to work, this policy risks ignoring broader economic conditions and structural inequalities. It shifts the burden of economic stability entirely onto individuals, rather than addressing systemic issues like labor market failures or inadequate public services that contribute to poverty.

Critics argue that job training does not address the root causes of economic instability, including wage stagnation and job scarcity. Many trained individuals still struggle to find stable, well-paying jobs due to a lack of sufficient employment opportunities. The problem is compounded by the fact that many vocational programs do not guarantee job placements, rendering the training ineffective if there are no available positions in the job market. According to recent insights, vocational and skills training programs have had mixed results, with some increasing employment chances and earnings only modestly (*Vocational and Skills Training Programs to Improve Labor Market Outcomes*, n.d.).

Furthermore, there is a risk of perpetuating cycles of poverty among marginalized populations by limiting their access to essential services. When social welfare policies neglect immediate financial assistance in favor of long-term employment training, they might inadvertently deepen economic disparities. Marginalized communities, which are often disproportionately affected by economic downturns, require continuous support to break free from poverty traps. Without a safety net, these communities could become further entrenched in poverty, as short-term needs are neglected in the pursuit of long-term goals.

Additionally, analysts highlight that the shift towards employment training can lead to a patchwork of unequal service availability. Local and state-level implementations of such programs often vary greatly, resulting in inconsistent support across different regions. This inconsistency can exacerbate existing inequalities, leaving individuals in less affluent areas with fewer resources and opportunities compared to those in more affluent regions.

Moreover, the success of employment training programs is highly dependent on the quality and comprehensiveness of the training provided. Programs that include practical experience, soft-skills training, and job referrals have shown more promise in improving employment outcomes. However, vocational training programs are often costly, ranging from a few hundred to more than US$10,000 per person, presenting a significant financial barrier for both individuals and the institutions responsible for implementing these programs (*Vocational and Skills Training Programs to Improve Labor Market Outcomes*, n.d.).

For policymakers, balancing immediate financial assistance with long-term employment training requires careful consideration. Strategies that combine both elements could offer a more holistic support system. For instance, providing initial financial stability through direct assistance can enable individuals to participate effectively in training programs without the distraction of immediate financial stress. Additionally, integrating supportive services such as childcare, transportation, and healthcare within training programs can help address the systemic barriers that prevent full participation in the workforce.

Evaluating the impact of such policy shifts on small businesses and entrepreneurs is also crucial. While large corporations might have the resources to implement extensive training programs, small businesses may struggle to provide similar opportunities due to limited funds. Ensuring that small businesses receive adequate support and incentives to participate in these training initiatives can foster a more inclusive and effective employment landscape.

Evaluating the economic policies detailed in Project 2025 reveals a noticeable shift toward promoting economic nationalism through social welfare reforms. By tightening eligibility requirements and emphasizing employment training over direct financial aid, these changes present a mixed bag of benefits and drawbacks. While the intent is to foster a self-reliant workforce, the reality is that marginalized communities may face increased barriers to necessary support. The risks include deepening existing inequalities and further marginalizing those who are already vulnerable, particularly when private sector solutions replace public welfare without adequate oversight or equitable access.

Furthermore, the implications for small businesses and entrepreneurs under Project 2025's economic nationalism are multifaceted. On one hand, prioritizing domestic industries could enhance national economic security; on the other, it imposes significant challenges on small enterprises dependent on global supply chains and international markets. Increased tariffs and stringent trade policies can inflate costs, making it harder for startups and small firms to compete. Additionally, the potential reduction in government-backed financial support in favor of private investment may hinder new entrepreneurs who lack substantial backing. Balancing these aspects is crucial for creating an inclusive economy where both individuals and small businesses can thrive amidst broader nationalistic goals.

Chapter 7: Environmental Policy Critique

Examining the environmental ramifications of Project 2025 reveals profound concerns about its potential to undermine decades of progress in climate initiatives and environmental protection regulations. This chapter delves into various proposed rollbacks, such as dismantling the Clean Air Act and repealing the Endangered Species Act, which pose significant threats to both ecosystems and public health. By analyzing these proposals, we can better understand the broader implications for air quality, species conservation, and water standards, illustrating how weakening these critical protections may lead to increased pollution and health risks for vulnerable populations.

Furthermore, the chapter explores the potential consequences of loosening regulations related to toxic waste disposal and water contamination, emphasizing the disproportionate impact on low-income and minority communities. It also considers the proposed withdrawal from international climate agreements like the Paris Agreement and the prioritization of fossil fuels over renewable energy sources. By evaluating these elements, the chapter provides a comprehensive critique of how Project 2025's policies could hinder global efforts to combat climate change and exacerbate existing social and environmental injustices. Through this examination, readers will gain insight into the far-reaching effects on public health, economic stability, and community well-being, highlighting the urgent need for continued advocacy to protect environmental and societal interests.

Proposals to Roll Back Environmental Regulations

Assessing the proposed rollbacks of existing environmental protections under Project 2025 reveals a series of changes that pose significant threats to both ecosystems and public health. One notable proposal involves dismantling the Clean Air Act, a cornerstone of American environmental policy since 1970. This legislation has been instrumental in reducing pollutants such as sulfur dioxide, carbon monoxide, and particulate matter, contributing to improved air quality and public health outcomes across the nation. However, Project 2025 aims to weaken these air quality standards, potentially leading to a substantial increase in pollutants.

The consequences of this rollback could be severe. Increased levels of pollutants are directly linked to respiratory illnesses, including asthma and chronic obstructive pulmonary disease (COPD). Vulnerable populations, such as children and the elderly, would face heightened risks, as their respiratory systems are particularly sensitive to poor air quality. The economic burden of healthcare costs associated with treating respiratory diseases would also likely rise, affecting families and communities across the country.

Another critical aspect of Project 2025 is the proposal to repeal the Endangered Species Act (ESA). Established in 1973, the ESA has played a crucial role in protecting species at risk of extinction, preserving biodiversity, and maintaining ecosystems' health and balance. By repealing this act, Project 2025 threatens to disrupt ecosystems profoundly. Species that are currently protected may face extinction, leading to cascading effects on food webs and ecosystem services. For example, the loss of pollinators like bees and butterflies could affect crop production and food security, impacting agricultural sectors and ultimately human nutrition.

Project 2025 also advocates for loosening water quality standards, which raises significant concerns about contamination risks. Water quality standards are fundamental in ensuring safe drinking water supplies and protecting aquatic habitats from pollution. Lowering these standards could result in higher levels of contaminants, such as heavy metals, pesticides, and industrial chemicals, entering water bodies. Communities relying on these water sources, especially those already facing economic or infrastructural challenges, would be at greater risk of exposure to harmful substances. This could lead to an increase in waterborne illnesses, such as gastrointestinal infections, and long-term health issues, including cancers and developmental disorders.

The weakening of regulations on toxic waste disposal is another alarming proposal within Project 2025. Current regulations aim to control the handling, treatment, and disposal of hazardous waste to minimize environmental and public health risks. Relaxing these regulations could encourage corporations to engage in harmful practices, further exacerbating environmental justice issues. Low-income and minority communities, which are often situated near industrial sites, would disproportionately bear the brunt of increased toxic waste exposure. These communities already experience higher instances of health problems linked to environmental pollutants, and reduced regulatory oversight would only deepen these inequities.

The broad implications of these rollbacks extend beyond immediate environmental and health impacts. They undermine decades of progress in environmental protection and set a dangerous precedent for future policy decisions. The enforcement mechanisms of key environmental regulations would be weakened, making it more difficult to hold polluters accountable. This erosion of regulatory frameworks not only endangers current ecosystems and public health but also compromises the ability to address emerging environmental challenges effectively.

For instance, the consolidation of scientific and policy decision-making under political appointees, as proposed by Project 2025, is particularly concerning. Such moves threaten the integrity of science-based policymaking at federal agencies like the Environmental Protection Agency (EPA). Political influence over scientific research and findings can lead to biased decisions that prioritize short-term economic gains over long-term environmental and public health benefits. Ensuring that policies are informed by rigorous, independent scientific research is essential for creating effective and sustainable environmental protections.

Furthermore, the plan's call to update the EPA's 2009 endangerment finding, which identifies greenhouse gas emissions as a threat to human health and the environment, could weaken or overturn this crucial determination. Revisiting this finding under political pressure could distort the scientific consensus on climate change and hinder efforts to mitigate its impacts. The inclusion of fewer pollutants and hazardous chemicals under regulatory scrutiny, as suggested by Project 2025, would leave many harmful substances unregulated, jeopardizing both environmental health and public safety.

Impact on Climate Change Initiatives

Project 2025 poses significant threats to critical climate change initiatives, potentially reversing years of progress in global environmental efforts. A central concern is its intent to withdraw the United States from international climate agreements, notably the Paris Agreement. The Paris Agreement has been a cornerstone for collaborative global action against climate change, aiming to limit global warming to well below 2 degrees Celsius. By pulling out of such agreements, Project 2025 would dismantle the collaborative framework that allows nations to coordinate their climate policies, share technologies, and assist each other in meeting their carbon reduction targets (Lespier et al., 2024). This withdrawal could set off a chain reaction where other countries may also retreat from their commitments, weakening the collective effort needed to combat climate change effectively.

In addition to severing ties with international agreements, Project 2025's prioritization of fossil fuels over renewable energy solutions is poised to exacerbate greenhouse gas emissions. Historical data and numerous studies have shown that fossil fuel combustion is a primary driver of carbon dioxide emissions, contributing significantly to global warming. According to Project 2025's proposals, there would be an intensified push for fossil fuel extraction and production, particularly across the Western Hemisphere (What Project 2025 Would Mean for Climate Change - Atmos, 2024). This approach starkly contrasts with the necessary shift towards renewable energy sources like wind, solar, and hydroelectric power, which are crucial for reducing carbon footprints. By sidelining renewable energy initiatives, Project 2025 could not only hinder the transition to cleaner energy but also lead to higher levels of air pollution and increased health risks associated with fossil fuel emissions.

A further alarming aspect of Project 2025 is its proposal to disband agencies dedicated to climate research and policy. Agencies such as the Environmental Protection Agency (EPA) play critical roles in collecting scientific data that informs climate policy and regulatory measures. The elimination of these agencies would significantly reduce the capacity for data-driven decision-making, leaving policymakers without the essential information needed to address climate challenges effectively (Lespier et al., 2024). Without robust scientific input, the development of effective climate strategies becomes increasingly difficult, leading to poorly informed decisions that may fail to mitigate environmental damage adequately.

Moreover, stifling demands for equity in climate action under Project 2025 perpetuates systemic inequalities and causes long-term harm to marginalized communities. Environmental justice initiatives like the Justice40 program aim to ensure that at least 40% of federal climate and clean energy investments benefit disadvantaged communities. These programs address the historical and disproportionate impact of environmental hazards on low-income and minority populations. Project 2025's agenda, which includes rolling back environmental justice initiatives, threatens to reverse this progress, leaving vulnerable communities exposed to pollution and climate risks without adequate support (What Project 2025 Would Mean for Climate Change - Atmos, 2024). The absence of equitable climate action exacerbates existing disparities, creating a scenario where the burden of environmental degradation falls more heavily on those already underrepresented.

The implications of Project 2025 extend beyond national borders, affecting global environmental efforts as well. For instance, the Biden-Harris administration reasserted U.S. leadership in climate action by rejoining the Paris Agreement and spearheading various international initiatives to combat climate change. These actions helped secure global commitments to transition away from fossil fuels and bolster support for clean energy projects worldwide (Lespier et al., 2024). In contrast, Project 2025 seeks to cut off funding for international climate initiatives and retract U.S. support for sustainable development globally. Such actions undermine international solidarity in addressing climate issues and could lead to a significant backslide in global emission reductions.

One clear example of the international impact of U.S. climate policy is the $43 million investment by the U.S. International Development Finance Corp. in mini-grid projects in India and Nigeria, aimed at reducing carbon emissions and improving access to clean electricity (Lespier et al., 2024). Projects like these demonstrate how U.S. involvement can foster economic growth and enhance resilience in developing countries. However, by ending support for such initiatives, Project 2025 not only jeopardizes these benefits but also weakens the global resolve to tackle climate change, increasing the risk of more severe climate impacts worldwide.

Furthermore, the recommendation to eliminate programs that safeguard public health and advance environmental justice reveals a disregard for the comprehensive nature of climate policies. Programs targeting environmental justice are crucial for mitigating risks in overburdened communities suffering from pollution and poor environmental conditions. Disbanding the EPA offices responsible for protecting these communities would disrupt efforts to monitor pollution and allocate funds for cleanup and mitigation (Lespier et al., 2024). This disruption would likely increase health disparities and environmental risks, particularly for Black, brown, Indigenous, and low-income populations. Consequently, the progress made toward securing safe and healthy communities for all would be undermined, leading to long-term detrimental effects on public health and societal wellbeing.

Project 2025's approach runs counter to the principles of sustainable development and environmental stewardship. Ignoring the necessity of transitioning to a low-carbon economy, the project promotes short-term economic gains at the expense of long-term environmental sustainability. The ramifications of such policies highlight the urgent need for continued advocacy and resistance to preserve the integrity of climate initiatives and protect vulnerable populations. By undermining critical climate change initiatives, Project 2025 poses a substantial threat not only to national interests but also to the broader global effort required to combat climate change successfully.

Broad Societal Impacts

Project 2025 poses significant societal implications, particularly in the realms of public health, economic stability, and community well-being. As we dive into these topics, it becomes evident that the far-reaching effects of this initiative could undermine substantial progress made in the environmental and public health sectors.

Starting with public health, one of the most alarming aspects of Project 2025 is its potential to increase healthcare costs driven by a rise in respiratory diseases caused by air pollution. The Environmental Protection Agency (EPA) has previously documented notable improvements in air quality, significantly reducing pollutants such as carbon monoxide and sulfur dioxide (Environmental Protection Agency, 2019). However, Project 2025 threatens to reverse these gains. By potentially easing regulations on industrial emissions, we can expect an uptick in airborne pollutants, leading to higher incidences of asthma, chronic bronchitis, and other respiratory conditions. For instance, fine particulate matter (PM2.5) and ozone have been linked to severe health outcomes, including premature deaths (Fuller, 2022). This surge in health issues will undoubtedly burden the healthcare system, escalating costs for treatments and hospital admissions.

Moreover, the economic ramifications of neglecting renewable energy opportunities are profound. Project 2025's focus on traditional fossil fuels over renewable energy sources not only perpetuates environmental degradation but also results in missed economic opportunities. The renewable energy sector, particularly wind and solar energy, has been a significant driver of job creation and economic growth in recent years. Failing to invest in these sectors means turning away from thousands of potential jobs and billions of dollars in economic output. This neglect also stifles innovation and competitiveness in the global market for clean energy technologies. Countries actively engaging in renewable energy investments are likely to outpace those clinging to outdated fossil fuel paradigms.

Public health is further threatened by contaminated water sources, especially near industrial sites. Water quality issues, often stemming from insufficient industrial regulations, disproportionately affect communities close to manufacturing facilities. These areas are at heightened risk for incidents of lead contamination and chemical runoff, which can infiltrate drinking water supplies. The Flint water crisis stands as a stark reminder of how catastrophic such contamination can be. Ingestion of pollutants like lead leads to serious health problems, including cognitive impairments in children and various chronic illnesses in adults. Without stringent regulatory oversight, Project 2025 could exacerbate these risks, leading to widespread public health crises.

Local governments, already grappling with existing pollution challenges, would face even greater hurdles under Project 2025. Municipalities would be tasked with addressing increased pollution without adequate federal support or stringent national regulations to fall back on. The EPA's role in monitoring and enforcing environmental standards is crucial; however, Project 2025's emphasis on deregulation undermines these efforts. Local governments would need to allocate more resources towards pollution control measures, straining budgets that might otherwise fund education, infrastructure, and social services. This strain is particularly pronounced in economically disadvantaged areas, where local administrations may lack the financial capacity to adequately combat pollution.

To illustrate the broader impact, consider the cumulative effect on a community living near an industrial site with relaxed environmental regulations. Residents might experience increased respiratory issues, leading to more frequent doctor visits and higher medical expenses. Concurrently, the local economy suffers from missed job opportunities in the burgeoning renewable energy sector. Furthermore, if the area's water supply becomes contaminated, the community faces additional health risks and costs associated with securing safe drinking water. Local government resources are stretched thin as officials strive to manage these compounded issues, ultimately detracting from other critical community services.

The societal implications of Project 2025 are stark and multifaceted. The increased healthcare costs due to rising air pollution-related respiratory diseases put immense pressure on both individuals and the healthcare system at large. The economic opportunity cost of neglecting the renewable energy sector translates into lost jobs and diminished economic growth. Public health crises from contaminated water supplies pose severe risks to community well-being, with long-term impacts that are difficult to quantify fully. Finally, overwhelmed local governments struggle to balance pollution control with other essential services, highlighting the broader systemic issues exacerbated by inadequate environmental policies.

Chapter 8: Education and Curriculum Changes

Education and curriculum changes are pivotal points of discussion in understanding how traditional values might reshape the current educational landscape. As educational philosophies shift towards these values, they propose significant modifications to the curricula, which focus on historical and literary works considered foundational. This emphasis aims to instill a sense of continuity and heritage within students. However, such transformations also pose questions about the inclusivity and breadth of perspectives offered in modern education.

In this chapter, we delve into the potential repercussions of aligning educational systems with traditional values, assessing their implications for both public schools and universities. The narrative explores how these proposed changes could realign curricula, implement standardized tests that prioritize factual recall, and establish training programs for educators rooted in traditional pedagogical methods. We also critically examine how these measures might affect inclusivity, academic freedom, and the overall quality of education, offering a comprehensive look at the multifaceted consequences of this shift.

Shift towards traditional values in education

An emphasis on traditional values in educational systems proposes a significant shift in how educational philosophies are shaped. Traditional values often focus on established norms and long-standing beliefs, which can potentially reshape curricula, moral and ethical development programs, standardized tests, and teacher training methods. While these changes aim to instill a sense of continuity and stability, they may also undermine critical thinking and inclusivity within the education sector.

One of the central proposed changes is a curriculum realignment that emphasizes classical literature and historical narratives reflecting traditional perspectives. Often, this involves a focus on works considered foundational to Western civilization, such as those by Shakespeare, Homer, and other classical authors. These texts are seen as vessels of timeless wisdom and moral guidance. However, critics argue that an exclusive focus on these works limits exposure to diverse voices and contemporary issues. By prioritizing canonical texts over modern and multicultural literature, students may miss out on a broader range of perspectives, leading to a narrow worldview that does not fully prepare them for a globally interconnected society.

The introduction of programs focusing on moral and ethical development based on traditional values is another area under consideration. Such initiatives often emphasize virtues like honor, duty, respect, and integrity, derived from longstanding cultural or religious traditions. For instance, character education programs might incorporate teachings from religious texts or historical figures celebrated for their moral uprightness. While promoting strong ethical principles is important, there is a risk that these programs can become prescriptive and dogmatic. Instead of fostering genuine ethical reasoning, they may encourage compliance with predefined moral codes, which can stifle independent thought and personal moral development (Gamage et al., 2021).

Furthermore, the implementation of standardized tests reflecting traditional values could prioritize rote memorization over analytical thinking. Standardized testing has always been a contentious issue, but aligning these tests with traditional values exacerbates concerns about their impact on student learning. Exams that focus heavily on factual recall rather than critical analysis promote a surface-level understanding of subjects. Students may excel at memorizing dates, names, and events without grasping their deeper significance or context. This approach to assessment runs counter to educational goals that emphasize critical thinking, problem-solving, and creativity—skills crucial for navigating complex modern challenges.

In addition to curricular and assessment changes, the development of training programs emphasizing traditional pedagogical methods could lead to more rigid teaching styles. Traditional approaches to pedagogy often involve direct instruction, where teachers impart knowledge, and students passively receive it. While there is value in structured learning environments, overly rigid adherence to these methods can suppress innovation and adaptability in the classroom. Educators trained exclusively in traditional techniques may be less equipped to engage students through interactive, student-centered learning experiences. This rigidity can hinder the development of critical thinking skills as students are not encouraged to question, explore, or contribute to their learning processes (American University, 2019).

Critically evaluating these proposed changes reveals a complex interplay between preserving valued traditions and adapting to contemporary educational needs. On one hand, grounding education in traditional values can provide students with a sense of heritage and continuity. It can foster respect for past achievements and reinforce societal norms that many consider foundational to moral and civic life. On the other hand, education must also prepare students to thrive in a rapidly evolving world. This requires exposure to diverse ideas, cultures, and viewpoints, which encourages critical reflection and open-mindedness.

Inclusivity is another crucial factor impacted by a shift towards traditional values in education. Modern educational philosophies increasingly recognize the importance of creating inclusive environments that honor and celebrate diversity. Curricula and programs designed with traditional values in mind may neglect or marginalize the experiences and contributions of various cultural, ethnic, and social groups. For example, a history curriculum focused solely on Western civilization overlooks the rich histories of non-Western societies, potentially alienating students from those backgrounds and failing to provide a comprehensive understanding of global history.

Moreover, traditional values-based programs might unwittingly enforce gender roles or exclude LGBTQ+ perspectives, affecting the inclusivity of moral and ethical education. Inclusivity in education means ensuring that all students see themselves reflected in the content they study and feel valued and respected in their learning environment. Therefore, while integrating traditional values into education, care must be taken to avoid reinforcing stereotypes or excluding marginalized groups.

The implications of these proposed modifications extend beyond the classroom. As graduates enter society, the type of education they receive profoundly influences their ability to engage as informed, thoughtful citizens. An education system that prioritizes traditional values at the expense of critical thinking and inclusivity risks producing individuals less prepared to address contemporary social issues. Instead of being equipped to challenge injustices and contribute to progressive change, students may emerge with limited perspectives and a diminished capacity for civic engagement.

Implications for public schools and universities

Changes in educational systems that prioritize traditional values have the power to significantly alter the landscape of public schools and higher education institutions. Such modifications can bring about a range of consequences, both immediate and long-term, affecting not only the students and faculty but also the broader society. Understanding these potential impacts is crucial for anyone concerned with the future of education, civic engagement, and social equity.

One of the primary ways these changes could manifest is through shifts in educational funding. If state or federal resources are reallocated to favor institutions that adhere strictly to traditional value systems, this could exacerbate existing inequities within the education system. Schools serving marginalized communities may find themselves at an even greater disadvantage if they do not comply with the prescribed value systems. These underfunded schools would struggle to provide quality education, leading to wider gaps in student achievements across different socio-economic backgrounds. The potential fallout here is significant: students from disadvantaged areas might receive a subpar education, further entrenching cycles of poverty and limiting upward mobility.

Another critical concern is the potential censorship of academic freedom. Censorship policies aimed at ensuring adherence to traditional values can create a chilling effect on research and academic discourse. Faculty members may feel pressured to avoid controversial topics or steer clear of lines of inquiry that could be perceived as challenging traditional norms. This restriction stifles intellectual diversity and hampers the exploration of contemporary issues that require innovative and critical thinking. As noted by the National Coalition Against Censorship (Southall, 2022), well-defined guidelines are essential to ensure that valuable knowledge is not withheld from students. Without clear policies, the risk of inconsistent application of censorship rules can lead to significant educational gaps, particularly in areas such as sexuality, race, and social justice.

The redefinition of student roles on campuses also emerges as a consequence of these educational changes. When institutional policies appear to infringe upon academic freedoms or personal rights, students may feel compelled to engage in activism and advocacy. Historical precedents show that campuses often become hotbeds for political movements when students perceive threats to their freedoms. This dynamic can either enrich the academic environment through robust debate and activism or create tension and division within the campus community. As students mobilize to protect their rights, the atmosphere may shift from one of academia-focused serenity to a battleground of ideologies.

Examining the long-term societal consequences reveals deeper implications. Graduates emerging from educational environments that limit exposure to diverse perspectives may harbor narrow views on critical social issues. This scenario jeopardizes the foundations of civic engagement and democratic participation as students lack the necessary skills and knowledge to critically analyze societal problems. Limiting discussions around topics such as race, gender, and sexuality can result in a generation less prepared to navigate and address the multifaceted challenges facing modern society. As articulated by the Intercultural Development Research Association (2022), censorship policies deprive students of the confidence and knowledge needed to engage in critical conversations, ultimately hindering their ability to act as informed and empathetic leaders in a democratic society.

Moreover, these traditional value-driven educational reforms can lead to homogenized curricular offerings that fail to reflect the diverse experiences and histories of all students. A curriculum focused predominantly on classical literature and historical narratives reflecting traditional values might overlook contributions from marginalized groups. This form of educational monoculture neglects the rich, multifaceted nature of American society and risks perpetuating systemic biases. By not acknowledging and integrating diverse viewpoints, the education system misses out on fostering a more inclusive and equitable learning environment.

The implications for educators cannot be understated either. Teachers find themselves caught between adherence to mandated curricula and the real educational needs of their students. With stringent restrictions placed on classroom content, educators may face penalties for violating policy, including losing their jobs or facing legal repercussions (Southall, 2022). This precarious position forces teachers to limit their engagement with students on crucial contemporary issues, thereby reducing the overall quality of education.

Furthermore, the societal ripple effects extend beyond the confines of individual schools. Communities that send their children to these traditional-value-oriented institutions may begin to see wider societal divides. Graduates who have been educated under restrictive curricula might enter the workforce and public life with limited skills in critical thinking and problem-solving.

Their narrowed worldview can influence various sectors, from business and politics to social services and community leadership, potentially stalling progress in addressing complex societal issues.

Insights and Implications

The proposed modifications to prioritize traditional values in educational systems present a complex set of implications for public schools and universities. These changes, if implemented, could reshape curricula, moral development programs, standardized tests, and teacher training methods, influencing not only the content taught but also the broader educational environment. While the emphasis on continuity and stability through classical literature and historical narratives seeks to uphold time-honored principles, it risks limiting the exposure students have to diverse perspectives. This narrowed focus may undermine critical thinking and inclusivity, essential components for preparing students to navigate an interconnected and evolving world.

Moreover, the socio-economic repercussions could be significant, particularly if funding shifts to favor institutions adhering to these traditional values. Marginalized communities might suffer from increased educational inequities, further entrenching cycles of poverty. Censorship and restrictions on academic freedom could stifle intellectual diversity, hindering research and discourse on contemporary issues. As graduates emerge from these reformed educational environments, their potential to engage as informed citizens and leaders may be compromised. Failing to address diverse viewpoints and contemporary challenges risks producing individuals ill-equipped to contribute meaningfully to societal progress and civic life.

Chapter 9: Healthcare Reforms Under Project 2025

Examining healthcare reforms is essential for understanding the future landscape of medical coverage and patient rights. Project 2025 presents a series of strategies that could significantly alter the current system established under the Affordable Care Act (ACA). The ACA has been a cornerstone in providing healthcare access to millions, especially those from vulnerable communities who benefited from expanded Medicaid and the elimination of lifetime coverage limits. However, proposed rollbacks detailed in Project 2025 aim to undo many of these advancements, posing serious risks to insurance market stability and individual healthcare security.

In this chapter, we will delve into the specifics of how potential rollbacks of the ACA could impact various facets of American healthcare. We will explore the possible financial and health consequences for low-income families and older adults who are most reliant on ACA provisions. Moreover, the chapter will analyze the larger implications of defunding organizations like Planned Parenthood, which provide critical reproductive health services beyond abortion. This review will also consider the broader societal repercussions, including increased healthcare costs and heightened disparities in health outcomes, particularly among marginalized communities. Through a thorough examination, this chapter aims to shed light on the far-reaching effects of Project 2025's healthcare proposals.

Potential Rollbacks of the Affordable Care Act

The Affordable Care Act (ACA), since its inception, has provided significant expansions in healthcare coverage and protections for vulnerable populations across the United States. One of its primary achievements has been reducing the number of uninsured individuals by offering subsidies to make private insurance more affordable and expanding Medicaid to low-income adults. The ACA also introduced essential health benefits and eliminated lifetime limits on coverage, providing a safety net for those who were previously unprotected.

Proposed rollbacks under Project 2025 threaten to undo these critical advancements, potentially reversing the insurance gains made under the ACA. These rollbacks could have severe consequences, especially for older adults and low-income families, who rely heavily on the protections and coverage facilitated by the ACA. Without these provisions, many may face increased financial burdens due to high medical expenses, leading to adverse health outcomes and economic instability.

The destabilization of insurance markets is another significant concern. If the proposed rollbacks are implemented, insurance premiums could skyrocket as insurers adjust to the reduced pool of enrollees. Higher premiums would place additional pressure on already financially strained households, forcing some to drop their coverage altogether. This shift would increase the number of uninsured individuals, creating a ripple effect throughout the healthcare system. The loss of coverage can lead to delayed treatment, worsened health conditions, and increased reliance on emergency services, which are costly and inefficient for both patients and healthcare providers.

Particularly alarming is the potential removal of preexisting condition protections. Under the ACA, insurers are prohibited from denying coverage or charging higher premiums based on an individual's medical history. This protection has been a lifeline for millions of Americans with chronic illnesses or past health issues, ensuring they receive the care they need without facing prohibitive costs. Removing these safeguards would leave millions vulnerable to discrimination in healthcare access, where insurers could deny crucial treatments or impose unaffordable premiums. This would disproportionately affect marginalized communities, exacerbating existing health disparities and perpetuating cycles of inequality.

The impact on social equity cannot be overstated. The ACA's expansions were particularly beneficial to people of color, who experienced larger coverage gains compared to their White counterparts. For instance, Medicaid expansion under the ACA has been pivotal in narrowing racial disparities in health coverage, contributing to improvements in access to care and health outcomes among Black and Hispanic communities. Repealing these expansions would likely widen these gaps again, resulting in greater barriers to healthcare, worsened health outcomes, and increased risk of medical debt for these groups. Specifically, the loss of Medicaid expansion could lead to disproportionate coverage losses among people of color, contributing to growing disparities in health outcomes and access to care (Loss of the Affordable Care Act Would Widen Racial Disparities in Health Coverage, 2020).

Moreover, the risks extend beyond individual health outcomes to broader societal implications. Health inequity is not only a moral issue but also an economic one. Poor health outcomes among vulnerable populations can lead to decreased productivity, higher absenteeism, and increased public spending on emergency and uncompensated care. By undermining healthcare access, Project 2025 could exacerbate these issues, leading to a less equitable and less productive society.

In the context of the ongoing COVID-19 pandemic, the importance of maintaining robust healthcare coverage becomes even more critical. The pandemic has disproportionately affected communities of color, highlighting the urgent need for accessible healthcare. Rolling back the ACA's provisions at such a time would be profoundly detrimental, leaving many without the necessary resources to combat the virus and its long-term effects.

One illustrative example comes from the Oregon Health Insurance Experiment, which studied the impact of Medicaid expansion through a lottery system. The research found that Medicaid coverage significantly increased outpatient visits, hospitalizations, and prescriptions while reducing depression prevalence and catastrophic medical expenditures (Baicker et al., 2013;

Finkelstein et al., 2012). Such findings underscore the positive impact that expanded healthcare access has on individual well-being and financial stability.

Furthermore, historical data shows that access to regular healthcare services, such as primary care, is associated with better health outcomes and lower healthcare costs. However, this access remains inequitable, with Black, Latino/a, AIAN, and other minoritized populations receiving lower-quality care compared to their White counterparts, even after adjusting for income and insurance coverage (Yearby et al., 2022). Public and rural hospital closures exacerbate this issue, particularly in areas with higher proportions of marginalized communities. Therefore, maintaining the protections and expansions under the ACA is crucial for advancing health equity and addressing systemic disparities in healthcare access.

Impact on Medicaid Expansion

Medicaid expansion has significantly enhanced health access for low-income individuals across many states. This initiative provided a safety net for millions of Americans who were previously without healthcare coverage, greatly improving their quality of life. By broadening eligibility criteria and increasing enrollment, Medicaid expansion enabled these individuals to receive essential medical services, including preventive and primary care. These improvements have been especially crucial in states that opted into the expansion, showcasing the tangible benefits of such policies.

However, the potential rollback of Medicaid expansion provisions poses a grave threat to these gains. Cuts to Medicaid funding could result in higher rates of untreated health issues among disadvantaged groups. Without access to affordable healthcare, many may forego necessary medical treatment, leading to worsened health conditions and increased hospitalizations. The absence of expansion could create barriers to accessing regular check-ups, medications, and specialist care, which are vital for managing chronic diseases and preventing severe health emergencies. If Medicaid is rolled back, we can expect a significant increase in both physical and mental health crises among those who rely on this program.

The moral implications of denying healthcare assistance to those most in need cannot be overstated. Healthcare is not merely a commodity but a fundamental human right. When society fails to provide healthcare support to its vulnerable members, it underscores deep ethical concerns about our collective responsibility to uphold social justice and equity. Denying Medicaid assistance exacerbates existing inequalities, disproportionately affecting marginalized communities that already face systemic barriers to obtaining healthcare. This ethical dilemma invites us to reconsider our priorities and advocate for policies that protect the well-being of all citizens, irrespective of their economic status.

One of the most compelling ways to understand the impact of Medicaid rollbacks is through personal stories. These narratives provide a human face to abstract numbers and statistics, illustrating the real-life consequences of policy changes. For example, consider Jane, a single mother living in a state that expanded Medicaid. With access to healthcare, she managed her diabetes effectively and maintained employment to support her family. However, if Medicaid provisions were rolled back, Jane might lose her coverage, making it difficult to afford insulin and doctor visits. The inevitable health decline could force her out of work, plunging her family into deeper financial instability and compromising her ability to care for her children.

Similarly, John, a middle-aged man with a heart condition, benefited from Medicaid when he lost his job during an economic downturn. The program allowed him to undergo crucial surgeries and follow-up treatments that saved his life. In a world where Medicaid is curtailed, individuals like John would face insurmountable medical bills or delayed treatment, severely jeopardizing their health outcomes. These stories highlight the indispensable role Medicaid plays in safeguarding public health and ensuring that every individual has the opportunity to live a healthy, productive life.

In states that have not expanded Medicaid, the consequences are already visible. According to research conducted by the University of Michigan and other institutions, states that expanded Medicaid saw improved health outcomes and reduced mortality rates compared to non-expansion states. The study revealed that Medicaid expansion saved 19,200 lives over four years, and if all states had implemented the program, an additional 15,600 deaths could have been averted (*Expanding Medicaid Can Save Lives*, 2019). The data underscores the life-saving potential of Medicaid expansion and raises critical questions about the moral cost of failing to provide it universally.

Furthermore, polls demonstrate strong public support for Medicaid expansion. A survey by KFF found that 75% of Americans viewed the ACA's Medicaid expansion favorably, and even in non-expansion states, 59% of residents expressed a desire for their state to adopt the program (*Expanding Medicaid Can Save Lives*, 2019). Despite this mandate, some lawmakers continue to resist expansion efforts, often citing budgetary constraints or ideological opposition. However, the arguments against expansion overlook the broader economic benefits, such as state budget savings and reduced uncompensated care costs for hospitals, especially in rural areas (Harker, 2024).

By examining the positive transformations witnessed in expansion states, it becomes evident that maintaining and furthering Medicaid expansion is not simply a political decision but a matter of public health necessity and social justice. If policymakers ignore these pressing realities and proceed with rollbacks, they risk reversing the progress made in recent years, leaving millions of Americans without critical health support and worsening existing health disparities.

Ultimately, the discussion around Medicaid expansion and potential rollbacks should focus on the tangible impacts on individuals' lives. Consider the story of Maria, a young woman recovering from substance abuse disorder. Through Medicaid, she accessed rehabilitation services that helped her regain control over her life. With proposed cuts, individuals like Maria might lose access to addiction treatment programs, increasing the likelihood of relapse and perpetuating cycles of poverty and poor health outcomes.

Defunding Planned Parenthood and Similar Organizations

Efforts to cut funding for organizations providing comprehensive reproductive health services are a significant concern under Project 2025. These organizations, such as Planned Parenthood, offer essential health services that go beyond abortion, including cancer screenings, testing and treatment for sexually transmitted infections, pap tests, cervical cancer screenings, family planning, birth control counseling, and sexuality education. For many low-income individuals, these services are often inaccessible elsewhere due to cost or lack of availability. Defunding these organizations would thus eliminate critical services that play a vital role in maintaining the health and well-being of millions, particularly those from marginalized communities.

Access to reproductive health services is fundamental to broader health equity. The Affordable Care Act (ACA) mandated that all contraceptive methods approved by the U.S. Federal Drug Administration be covered by insurance without cost sharing, significantly reducing out-of-pocket expenses for women. Eliminating funding for organizations that provide these services would exacerbate health disparities, especially for low-income women, women of color, young women, and immigrant women. These groups rely heavily on federal programs like Title X and Medicaid, which currently support comprehensive reproductive health care through organizations like Planned Parenthood. Any cuts to these programs would disproportionately affect the most vulnerable populations, widening existing health inequities.

Historical trends reveal a persistent push to defund reproductive health services, often tied to broader movements seeking to deprioritize women's health rights. For instance, past efforts to defund Planned Parenthood have been based largely on its provision of abortion services, even though abortion accounts for only about 3 percent of its total services (Taylor, 2017-01-18). This historical context is crucial for understanding current legislative proposals and their potential impact. These proposals not only threaten access to abortion but also undermine the overall autonomy of women over their reproductive health.

Legislative proposals to restrict abortion access pose a considerable threat to reproductive autonomy and increase health risks for women. Abortion bans and restrictions are not just cultural or religious issues; they have tangible economic and health consequences. According to Banerjee (2023), abortion access directly impacts labor market experiences and economic outcomes, with denial leading to prolonged financial distress and lower-paying jobs. Reproductive health restrictions limit a woman's ability to make decisions about her body and future, which can lead to increased unintended pregnancies and associated health risks.

Abortion access is intertwined with economic progress and mobility. Studies show that states with strict abortion laws tend to have weaker labor standards and underfunded public services, contributing to the economic subjugation of women (Banerjee, 2023). In turn, limited access to reproductive health services can trap women in cycles of poverty and economic dependence. For example, denying access to abortion has been linked to lower educational attainment and career outcomes, particularly affecting black and Hispanic women who already face steep economic disadvantages.

Furthermore, the rollback of ACA provisions and the defunding of organizations like Planned Parenthood would result in higher healthcare costs for women. The ACA's benefits extend beyond physical health, enabling women to save money on preventive care and contraception, which can then be used for other household expenses. Repealing these benefits would increase out-of-pocket costs, forcing many families to forgo necessary health services. This rollback would particularly hit hard on women of color and low-income women, exacerbating existing health disparities and economic inequities.

The moral implications of denying healthcare assistance to those most in need cannot be overlooked. Restricting access to reproductive health services raises serious ethical concerns about social justice and equality. It is essential to recognize that comprehensive reproductive health care is a basic human right that should be accessible to all, regardless of socio-economic status. By scaling back funding for these services, policymakers compromise the health and autonomy of countless women, undermining their capacity to lead productive and fulfilling lives.

Examining personal stories illustrates the real-life consequences of defunding reproductive health services. Many women share experiences of how access to Planned Parenthood and similar organizations enabled them to receive life-saving treatments and preventive care otherwise out of reach. These narratives highlight the indispensable role such organizations play in promoting public health and underscore the devastating impact of funding cuts. Communities that benefit from these services often lack alternative options, making the proposed defunding even more detrimental.

Access to Family Planning Services

Restricting access to birth control and family planning options can have far-reaching consequences on women's educational and economic opportunities. When women cannot plan and space their pregnancies, unintended pregnancies become more common, which can interfere with their educational goals. College completion rates drop, and career aspirations often get sidelined. The impact extends beyond individual ambitions; it affects entire communities as women contribute significantly to economic growth and stability. Studies have shown that women who can delay childbearing until they finish their education tend to secure better employment opportunities and earn higher wages throughout their careers. Consequently, limiting access to reproductive health services not only stalls individual progress but also curtails the potential for broader social and economic development.

Data consistently shows how limited access to family planning impacts various socioeconomic groups disproportionately. The burden falls more heavily on low-income women and women of color. For example, a study indicated that Black and Hispanic women were more likely than White women to receive counseling about sterilization, reflecting a disconcerting pattern of coercive practices (Dehlendorf et al., 2010). Moreover, an estimated 19 million women in the U.S. live in contraceptive deserts—areas where there is little or no availability of a full range of FDA-approved contraceptive methods (Simhoni, 2024). Women in these areas face systemic barriers such as inadequate transportation, financial constraints, and lack of childcare when seeking birth control. These hurdles perpetuate cycles of poverty and limit the upward mobility of these disadvantaged groups.

Reproductive health is deeply intertwined with broader themes of social justice and equality. Access to contraception empowers women to make informed choices about their bodies and futures, thereby contributing to gender equality. Without access to reliable family planning, women are at a higher risk of experiencing unwanted pregnancies, which can lead to unsafe abortions and related health complications. Historically marginalized communities have faced numerous challenges in accessing adequate reproductive healthcare. Structural racism and historical unethical practices in the development of contraception have eroded trust in the healthcare system. For instance, nearly 70,000 people, predominantly women of color, were coerced into sterilization during the 20th century (Simhoni, 2024). Recognizing and addressing these injustices is crucial for fostering a healthcare environment where all women feel respected and supported in their reproductive choices.

Limiting educational initiatives reduces awareness and access to crucial health information, which further compounds the problem. Comprehensive sex education plays a vital role in teaching young people about contraception and safe sexual practices. When educational initiatives are restricted, misinformation flourishes, leading to risky behaviors and unintended pregnancies. Moreover, without proper education, many individuals may not be aware of the reproductive health services available to them or how to access these services effectively. Public information campaigns have been effective in promoting other health outcomes, like tobacco cessation, and could similarly improve understanding and use of contraceptive methods if they were adequately funded and implemented. Ensuring culturally appropriate and accessible information reaches underserved communities is essential for improving public health.

The potential limitations on birth control and family planning options have significant implications for both individual lives and societal wellbeing. Restricting access leads to higher rates of unintended pregnancies, which hinder women's educational and economic prospects. Disparities in access to reproductive health care exacerbate existing socioeconomic inequalities, particularly affecting low-income and minority women (Dehlendorf et al., 2010). Reproductive health is intrinsically linked to issues of social justice, making it imperative to address these disparities. Comprehensive sex education and public awareness initiatives are crucial to improving outcomes and ensuring that all women, regardless of their background, have the knowledge and resources to make informed decisions about their reproductive health.

Chapter 10: National Security and Immigration Policies

National security and immigration policies intersect in ways that significantly shape the landscape of civil liberties and social equity. The proposed changes presented within Project 2025 highlight an authoritarian approach to governance, using stringent immigration enforcement as a cornerstone. The increase in border patrol funding, criminalization of asylum seekers, and enhanced surveillance technologies are central components contributing to this narrative. By examining these elements, one can understand how they reinforce control and restriction, overshadowing humanitarian concerns and freedoms traditionally valued in democratic societies.

Throughout this chapter, the implications of heightened border patrol funding will be explored, illustrating its dual role in national security and the potential erosion of civil rights. The discussion will then move on to the troubling trend of criminalizing asylum seekers, fundamentally altering the perception and treatment of individuals seeking refuge. Additionally, the deployment of advanced surveillance technologies raises critical questions regarding privacy and discrimination, with a significant focus on the broader socio-political consequences. Finally, the impact of these policies on refugee admissions will be assessed, highlighting a shift towards isolationism and its ramifications for both national identity and global humanitarian efforts. This analytical review aims to provide a comprehensive understanding of how these policy changes serve an overarching authoritarian agenda.

Stricter Immigration Enforcement

This subpoint examines how stricter immigration policies bolster the authoritarian narrative, illustrating its implications for civil liberties and social equity.

Increase in Border Patrol Funding

The increase in funding for border patrol initiatives is a critical component of the proposed immigration changes. The government's budgetary allocations reflect a shift towards stringent border enforcement mechanisms. This increase is viewed as essential to fortifying national security; however, it also raises questions about the impact on civil liberties. Higher financial investment in border control often translates into an expanded presence of law enforcement at national borders. This can lead to heightened surveillance and increased interactions between border agents and migrants, many of whom may face invasive questioning or detention without due process (American Immigration Council, 2023).

For instance, during the Trump administration, there was a significant hike in the budget for Customs and Border Protection (CBP), which included funds for additional personnel and advanced technological equipment such as drones and biometric systems. These measures are framed as necessary to combat illegal immigration and secure the nation's borders. However, this approach often criminalizes undocumented migrants and asylum seekers, portraying them as threats to national security rather than individuals fleeing persecution and violence.

Moreover, funneling resources into border patrol operations diverts funds from other areas that could address the root causes of migration, such as international aid or economic development programs in migrant-sending countries. This reallocation of resources underscores an enforcement-first mentality, which prioritizes immediate deterrence over long-term solutions to migration issues. Such policies contribute to an authoritarian narrative by emphasizing control and restriction over humanitarian considerations and social equity.

Criminalization of Asylum Seekers

A particularly troubling aspect of the proposed immigration policies is the criminalization of asylum seekers. Current proposals suggest classifying asylum-seeking as a criminal act, thus subjecting individuals to legal penalties simply for attempting to seek refuge. This approach fundamentally alters the principle of asylum, which is grounded in international human rights law that recognizes the right to seek protection from persecution (Wasem, 2020).

The Trump administration's "zero tolerance" policy, for example, mandated the prosecution of all illegal border crossers, leading to the widespread separation of families and detention of asylum seekers. This policy not only caused significant human suffering but also sent a clear message: seeking asylum would no longer be treated as a humanitarian issue, but rather as a criminal act.

Such measures create a climate of fear among potential asylum seekers, deterring them from exercising their rights under international law. It also undermines America's historical role as a haven for those escaping oppression. Criminalizing asylum seekers reinforces a punitive immigration system that prioritizes exclusion over protection, aligning with authoritarian tendencies that seek to limit rights and freedoms.

Moreover, this criminalization disproportionately affects vulnerable groups, including children and those fleeing gender-based violence or political persecution. By treating these individuals as criminals, the policies exacerbate social inequities and erode the principles of justice and compassion that underpin democratic societies.

Enhanced Surveillance Technologies

The deployment of enhanced surveillance technologies for monitoring immigrant populations is another key aspect of the stricter immigration policies. These technologies include facial recognition software, biometric databases, and advanced tracking systems designed to monitor and manage the movement of immigrants within the country.

While proponents argue that these tools are necessary for maintaining national security and ensuring compliance with immigration laws, they also pose significant risks to privacy and civil liberties. Enhanced surveillance technologies can lead to intrusive monitoring practices that target specific communities based on race, ethnicity, or immigration status. This targeting not only discriminates against certain groups but also fosters a climate of suspicion and mistrust (Wasem, 2020).

For instance, the use of facial recognition technology at airports and border checkpoints has raised concerns about accuracy and bias. Studies have shown that these systems are often less accurate in identifying individuals with darker skin tones, leading to higher rates of false positives and misidentifications. Such errors can result in unjust detentions and other legal consequences for innocent individuals, further entrenching systemic inequities.

Additionally, the accumulation of vast amounts of personal data through biometric systems poses risks of misuse and unauthorized access. Without robust data protection measures and oversight, there is a danger that this information could be exploited for purposes beyond immigration enforcement, such as mass surveillance of the general population. This erosion of privacy rights aligns with broader authoritarian trends that prioritize state control and oversight over individual freedoms.

Impact on Refugee Admissions

Finally, the impact of stricter immigration policies on refugee admissions is profound. Proposals to reduce the number of refugees admitted to the United States reflect a departure from the country's tradition of offering sanctuary to those in need. This shift is emblematic of an inward-looking, isolationist stance that prioritizes national interests over global humanitarian responsibilities.

The Trump administration implemented drastic cuts to refugee admissions, setting historically low caps on the number of refugees allowed into the country. These reductions were justified using national security rhetoric, despite evidence that refugees undergo extensive vetting processes before being admitted. Such policies not only diminish America's standing as a leader in humanitarian efforts but also leave countless individuals in precarious situations without the possibility of resettlement.

Reducing refugee admissions has several implications. First, it exacerbates the plight of those fleeing conflict, persecution, and natural disasters, leaving them with few viable options for safety and stability. Second, it undermines international solidarity and burden-sharing, as fewer countries may feel compelled to uphold their commitments to refugee protection. Third, it perpetuates xenophobic narratives that portray refugees as threats rather than contributors to society.

These policies also have broader implications for social equity. Refugees often bring diverse skills and perspectives that enrich their host communities. By closing the door on refugees, the United States misses out on the potential benefits of their contributions, further entrenching societal divisions and inequities.

Enhanced Surveillance Technologies

One of the core components of modern immigration enforcement is the utilization of advanced surveillance technologies. Leveraging sophisticated tools, authorities can now monitor immigrant activities with unprecedented precision and reach. These technological advances come in many forms, including drones, biometric systems, facial recognition software, and automated license plate readers. Each technology presents unique capabilities to track and gather data on individuals crossing borders or residing in the country without proper documentation. However, while these tools enhance the efficiency of monitoring activities, they also provoke serious questions regarding privacy and civil rights.

In recent years, governments have increasingly relied on technologies such as facial recognition to identify and detain undocumented immigrants. This development has sparked a significant debate over the potential infringement on personal privacy and constitutional rights. Facial recognition systems, for instance, utilize algorithms to match captured images against databases, potentially leading to false positives and subsequent wrongful detentions. Additionally, there are concerns about the scope of data collection and how this information is stored and used. Critics argue that mass data collection efforts disregard fundamental privacy principles enshrined in various laws, creating an environment where personal freedoms could be eroded without sufficient legal protections (Lee & Chin, 2022).

The normalization of surveillance technologies raises another critical issue: the evolution of a surveillance culture. As surveillance becomes more embedded in everyday life, it risks fostering an atmosphere of constant monitoring and self-censorship. Individuals, aware of being watched, may alter their behaviors, leading to a chilling effect on free speech and expression. For immigrant communities, the impact is particularly acute. Living under constant watch can exacerbate feelings of marginalization and fear, discouraging them from participating fully in public life. This pervasive sense of surveillance undermines trust between immigrant communities and law enforcement agencies, making it harder to foster cooperative relationships essential for community safety and cohesion.

Moreover, understanding the implications of technological surveillance extends beyond privacy concerns to broader questions about authoritarian control. History has shown that increased surveillance capabilities often coincide with trends toward more authoritarian governance. Surveillance technology not only enables governments to monitor individuals more efficiently but also to suppress dissent and control populations. By enhancing the state's ability to track and manage people's movements and communications, these technologies empower authorities to enforce compliance and silence opposition more effectively.

A poignant example of this trend can be observed in the deployment of drones for border surveillance. Drones equipped with high-resolution cameras and sensors patrol vast stretches of the border, capturing real-time data on anyone attempting to cross. While effective for border security, this technology also means that individuals in border regions live under constant observation. Such measures can be seen as stepping stones toward more intrusive state control, wherein the line between national security and the infringement of individual liberties becomes increasingly blurred.

Furthermore, biometric systems represent another front in the battle between security and privacy. These systems, which include fingerprinting, iris scanning, and DNA profiling, offer precise methods of identifying individuals. However, the aggregation of biometric data poses heightened risks if abused or improperly secured. Unauthorized access or misuse of such sensitive information can lead to severe consequences, including identity theft, discrimination, and unjust persecution. The reliability of these systems is also questionable, given that even minor errors can result in significant hardships for those misidentified.

Additionally, the adoption of automated license plate readers (ALPRs) accentuates the complexity of balancing surveillance with civil liberties. ALPRs capture and store vehicle movement data across extensive networks, facilitating real-time tracking of individuals' travel patterns. This capability aids in apprehending criminals and managing traffic but simultaneously builds comprehensive logs of innocent citizens' whereabouts. Concerns arise when such data is retained indefinitely or shared across multiple government agencies, creating the potential for abuse and unauthorized access.

Advocating for robust oversight mechanisms is essential to address these privacy concerns and mitigate the risks associated with surveillance technologies. Reform proposals include establishing clear guidelines on the permissible use of surveillance tools, mandating transparency in data collection practices, and implementing measures to ensure accountability. For instance, requiring judicial authorization for certain surveillance activities can help prevent unwarranted intrusions into private lives. Auditing processes and independent review boards can further bolster safeguards, ensuring that surveillance practices comply with legal and ethical standards.

Military Spending and Defense Policies

Increased military spending and aggressive defense policies play a significant role in reinforcing an authoritarian framework by prioritizing militarization over societal needs. By channeling vast resources into the Department of Defense, Project 2025 reflects a shift towards prioritizing state security and control at the expense of public welfare programs such as healthcare, education, and social services.

The proposed budget increases for the Department of Defense are substantial. These financial augmentations are often justified on the grounds of national security, citing threats both foreign and domestic. However, this justification serves a dual purpose: not only does it address real or perceived external dangers, but it also lays the groundwork for a more centralized and unassailable governmental power. For example, Congress has seen proposals requesting additional billions for advanced weapon systems, cybersecurity initiatives, and expanded troop deployments. The funds allocated for these purposes come at the cost of underfunding essential social services that directly impact the quality of life of citizens. This imbalance underscores a governance style that values military might over societal well-being.

The rhetoric used to justify military actions abroad further reinforces this trend. Proponents emphasize terms like "preemptive strikes" and "defending democracy," which create an environment where perpetual military engagement is normalized. Such appeals to security offer a veneer of legitimacy to interventions, making them seem necessary and beneficial. Yet, these justifications often obscure the underlying motives, such as projecting power or securing strategic interests rather than addressing immediate threats. This strategic narrative engenders a culture of fear and dependence on military solutions, thus bolstering authoritarian tendencies by rallying public support around the notion of an ever-present threat that only a strong, militarized government can counter.

Legislation supporting increased surveillance is another critical component of this framework. Policies that expand surveillance capabilities inch closer to martial law-like conditions, where the civil liberties of citizens are compromised under the guise of national security. For instance, laws have been enacted to allow broader data collection and monitoring of personal communications without substantial judicial oversight. This shift mirrors military intelligence operations and creates an atmosphere where privacy is sacrificed for the illusion of safety. The implications of such policies are profound, as they facilitate a state apparatus that can suppress dissent and monitor opposition, core characteristics of an authoritarian regime.

The militarization of local police forces ties directly into these broader themes. Policies encouraging collaboration between the military and local law enforcement result in police departments acquiring surplus military equipment, such as armored vehicles and high-caliber weapons. This trend transforms community policing into quasi-military operations, fundamentally altering the relationship between police and the communities they serve. For instance, programs like the Department of Defense’s 1033 Program have enabled local police to access military-grade gear, ostensibly for counter-terrorism purposes. However, the presence of such equipment during routine policing activities has escalated tensions, leading to incidents where the line between military and civilian operations is blurred.

This militarization extends beyond equipment; it also influences tactics and training. Police officers trained in military techniques are more likely to employ forceful measures, contributing to a cycle of violence and mistrust. In essence, local law enforcement agencies become extensions of the military, exercising control through intimidation and force rather than community engagement and problem-solving. This evolution supports an authoritarian agenda by ensuring that mechanisms of state violence are ubiquitous and ready to quell any form of resistance or civil unrest swiftly and decisively.

The intertwining of increased military spending, aggressive defense policies, expanded surveillance, and the militarization of local police forces portrays a society progressively leaning towards authoritarianism. The emphasis on militarization systematically diverts focus from addressing societal needs and erodes democratic norms by concentrating power within state security structures. As this framework takes hold, the capacity for meaningful civic participation diminishes, paving the way for a more controlled and less accountable form of governance.

Impact on Refugee Admissions

Strict immigration enforcement policies that propose reductions in refugee admissions have a profound ethical, national identity, and humanitarian implications. This subpoint delves into these dimensions, unpacking the moral considerations, impacts on American historical roles, long-term international repercussions, and the consequences of reducing refugee admittance numbers.

Ethical Considerations:
Turning away refugees raises critical ethical questions. Refugees often flee war, persecution, and dire economic conditions with no safe alternatives. The United States has historically been a land of refuge, enshrining protections through legislative action such as the Refugee Act of 1980. By significantly curtailing refugee admissions, we deny sanctuary to vulnerable individuals, potentially condemning them to suffering or death. Such policies conflict with humanitarian principles and international commitments, highlighting a stark moral dilemma.

National Identity:
Refugee admissions are deeply intertwined with themes of American identity. The nation's historical narrative is rich with stories of immigrants seeking safety and opportunity, contributing to its cultural and economic fabric. Limiting refugee intake contradicts this legacy, promoting an exclusionary vision contrary to the foundational values of freedom and open arms. These measures risk eroding the diverse, inclusive character that defines America, steering it towards isolationism and cultural stagnation.

Long-term Repercussions:
The ripple effects of reduced refugee admissions extend far beyond domestic borders. Internationally, America's leadership in humanitarian efforts sets a precedent for other nations. Drastically lowering admissions can undermine global humanitarian initiatives, damaging diplomatic relationships and diminishing the country's standing as a protector of human rights. Furthermore, this stance could weaken collaborative efforts to address global crises, leading to increased instability and regional conflicts, ultimately affecting global peace and security.

Refugee Admittance Reduction:
The proposed cuts to refugee admissions under strict immigration policies present concerning outcomes. A notable aspect is the sheer reduction in annual quotas. During previous administrations, the ceiling for refugee admissions witnessed significant decreases, with numbers dropping from a high of over 100,000 to around 15,000 in recent years. Such reductions disregard the growing displacement crises worldwide.

The immediate consequences include leaving thousands in precarious situations, unable to find safety. These policies also strain neighboring countries bearing the burden of large refugee populations, potentially destabilizing entire regions. Domestically, reducing refugee numbers affects communities that have benefited from their contributions, both economically and culturally.

Chapter 11: State vs Federal Powers

The balance of power between state and federal governments is an ever-evolving aspect of American governance, one which significantly shapes the political landscape. This chapter delves into how shifts in this balance can redefine the roles of state governments and influence authority distribution within the United States. By examining historical precedents, key legal frameworks, and contemporary political motivations, readers will gain a nuanced understanding of how these shifts impact governance at both state and national levels.

Throughout the chapter, the analysis will focus on several critical dimensions. Historical contexts such as the Articles of Confederation and pivotal judicial decisions will be explored to trace the cyclical nature of American federalism. The examination will also extend to legal frameworks like the Tenth Amendment and recent Supreme Court rulings that underscore state autonomy. Additionally, the chapter will discuss the political and social ramifications of shifting powers, assessing how state policies can diverge from federal objectives and affect civil liberties. Finally, implications for state-level policy-making, including potential benefits and risks, will be considered, providing a thorough exploration of this complex and dynamic facet of governance.

Potential Shift of Powers to State Governments

The balance of power between state and federal governments in the United States has always been a dynamic and evolving aspect of American governance. Understanding how periodic shifts of power to state governments can redefine their role in governance and influence the balance of authority is crucial for both politically active individuals and scholars alike.

Historical Precedents of State Power

One of the most prominent characteristics of American federalism has been its cyclical nature, where periods of centralized federal power are often followed by phases emphasizing state authority. Historical instances reveal this ebb and flow. For example, during the early years of the Republic, the Articles of Confederation provided substantial powers to the states with minimal federal oversight. This period highlighted the challenges of a weak central government, leading to the drafting and adoption of the Constitution in 1787, which created a more balanced distribution of powers.

The debates between Federalists and Anti-Federalists further cemented the significance of state authority. The Federalist era (1789-1801), particularly under Alexander Hamilton, saw significant federal consolidation, whereas Thomas Jefferson's presidency marked a shift towards strengthening state powers. Similarly, the concept of "dual federalism," prevalent in the 19th century, supported distinct and separate spheres of influence for state and federal governments.

Cases like Gibbons v. Ogden (1824) initially reinforced federal supremacy but also acknowledged states' rights within their jurisdictions.

Legal Framework and Binding Conventions

The legal framework governing state and federal powers is rooted in the U.S. Constitution and subsequent amendments. The Tenth Amendment explicitly reserves to the states any powers not delegated to the federal government, underscoring the significance of state authority. Key constitutional provisions, such as the Supremacy Clause, establish federal law as the "supreme Law of the Land," but judicial interpretations have continuously shaped the practical application of these laws.

Recent legal decisions indicate a trend toward empowering state governance. For instance, several Supreme Court rulings have reaffirmed states' rights in various domains. In Printz v. United States (1997), the Court held that the federal government could not command state officials to enforce federal regulations, emphasizing states' autonomy. Similarly, cases like NFIB v. Sebelius (2012) allowed states to opt-out of federal Medicaid expansion mandates, highlighting the limits of federal coercion over state policy choices.

Such rulings signal a broader jurisprudential trend favoring state sovereignty. However, it is essential to recognize that while the courts provide certain protections for state authority, they also impose constraints to ensure a balance that upholds national coherence.

Political Will and Agenda

The political motivations behind the transfer of power to states are multifaceted, often reflecting broader ideological battles within American politics. Conservative movements, in particular, have been vocal advocates for increased state powers. Libertarian ideologies emphasize minimal federal intervention and greater local control. This view aligns with historical conservative principles advocating for a smaller federal government and more robust state governance.

The resurgence of states' rights discourse can be observed in contemporary policy debates, especially around issues such as healthcare, education, and environmental regulation. For instance, during the Obama administration, conservative states sought to resist federal initiatives, such as the Affordable Care Act, pushing for state-level alternatives. This resistance was often framed as a defense of local autonomy against perceived federal overreach.

Moreover, the political landscape shapes how states utilize newfound powers. States with conservative leadership may implement policies diverging significantly from those of liberal states, leading to potential conflicts with federal objectives. These dynamics underscore the complex interplay between state agendas and national priorities, revealing the intricate nature of American federalism.

Implications for Civil Liberties

Shifting powers to state governments can have profound implications for civil liberties, particularly concerning minority rights and freedoms. Historical and contemporary examples reveal that state autonomy can both protect and undermine individual rights, depending on the prevailing political context and social attitudes.

A notable historical precedent is the Civil Rights Movement, where federal intervention was crucial in dismantling segregation and ensuring equal rights for African Americans. Landmark decisions like Brown v. Board of Education (1954) and the enforcement of the Voting Rights Act of 1965 exemplify instances where federal authority was necessary to guarantee civil liberties against state-sanctioned discrimination.

However, the current trend toward enhancing state powers raises concerns about the potential erosion of civil liberties. For example, recent legislative efforts in various states to restrict voting rights, regulate reproductive health, and limit LGBTQ+ protections highlight the risks associated with increased state autonomy. Such measures often disproportionately affect marginalized communities, exacerbating existing inequalities.

Furthermore, the debate surrounding the Establishment Clause presents another dimension of this issue. Some scholars argue that applying the Establishment Clause to states constrains religious freedom, while others contend that it is essential to prevent state-endorsed religion. Despite differing viewpoints, the prohibition of state religious establishments remains a critical safeguard for religious liberty, protected both by historical interpretation and the Free Exercise Clause (Chapman & Yoshino, 2023).

Impact on State-Level Policy Making

Empowering states to craft their policies can lead to a substantial variation in laws across the country. This decentralization allows states to create tailored solutions for their unique demographics and circumstances but also risks creating a patchwork of regulations that could impact national unity and the citizen experience. Citizens moving from one state to another may find starkly different legal landscapes and social norms. For instance, differing state laws on issues such as healthcare, education, and drug legalization could cause confusion and inconvenience for individuals and businesses operating in multiple states. These disparities might foster a sense of division rather than cohesion among Americans.

Variations in state policies also have implications for national programs and standards. For example, educational systems vary significantly between states, leading to unequal opportunities and outcomes for students nationwide. While some states may excel by implementing innovative teaching methods or curricula, others might lag due to inadequate funding or outdated practices. This inconsistency can perpetuate inequality and limit upward mobility for students in underperforming regions. Additionally, environmental laws are often more stringent in some states compared to others, creating challenges for addressing climate change uniformly across the nation.

As states gain more power, local governments have the opportunity to address community-specific needs more effectively. Strategic local governance enables these governments to implement policies that reflect the values and experiences of their populations. States like California and Oregon, for example, have pioneered progressive environmental regulations that have set benchmarks for other states and even influenced federal policy. By allowing local leaders to be more responsive to their constituents' needs, states can become laboratories of democracy where new ideas are tested and successful policies are adopted elsewhere (Simon et al., 2018).

However, strategic local governance requires accountability and transparency to operate successfully. Decentralized power can sometimes lead to reduced oversight and increased potential for corruption or inefficiency. When state governments enact legislation that diminishes checks and balances, it becomes harder for citizens to hold their leaders accountable. Transparency issues can particularly harm disenfranchised communities that already struggle with limited political influence. For example, some states have passed laws making it more difficult for marginalized groups to vote, which can undermine democratic principles and weaken trust in the political system.

To mitigate these risks, states should establish clear guidelines for maintaining accountability and transparency. This includes ensuring robust checks and balances within state governments, promoting open access to government data, and fostering active civic engagement. By upholding these standards, states can build trust among their residents and ensure that power is exercised responsibly.

The long-term consequences of a shift toward state power could reshape the federalist model in the U.S. Federalism was originally designed to balance power between the national government and the states, allowing for both unity and diversity. If the trend toward decentralized power continues, we may witness a transformation in how this balance is maintained. Future legislative battles may revolve around which level of government has the authority to regulate various aspects of American life. The role of the Supreme Court could become increasingly significant as it interprets the constitutionality of state versus federal powers.

This evolving dynamic could influence broader governance practices. States may push back against federal mandates they perceive as overreaching, while the federal government may attempt to assert its authority in areas like healthcare, education, and environmental protection. This tug-of-war between state and federal powers will likely shape the political landscape for years to come, affecting everything from economic policy to civil liberties.

Political and Social Ramifications

Throughout American history, the balance between state and federal powers has been a contentious issue that significantly influences politics and society. Examining various historical instances reveals how this tension shapes contemporary political landscapes.

One of the earliest examples of this tug-of-war is the Nullification Crisis in the 1830s, where South Carolina attempted to nullify federal tariffs, asserting state sovereignty over federal mandates. This standoff underscored the ongoing struggle for power between states and the federal government. Similarly, during the Civil Rights Movement of the 1960s, the federal government had to intervene in state policies to ensure the protection of civil rights, as states like Alabama resisted desegregation efforts. These historical episodes highlight how the tension between state and federal powers can lead to significant political and social upheavals, influencing current debates on governance and policy-making.

In recent years, there has been a noticeable trend toward decentralizing power, as evidenced by several legal decisions aimed at reinvigorating federalism. For instance, landmark rulings such as United States v. Lopez (1995) and National Federation of Independent Business v. Sebelius (2012) have bolstered state authority by limiting the scope of federal power under the Commerce Clause and the Affordable Care Act, respectively. These decisions suggest a judicial inclination to reallocate certain responsibilities back to the states, impacting civil liberties and individual rights. The shift towards decentralized governance raises questions about uniformity in civil protections and the potential for states to either safeguard or undermine these liberties based on local priorities (States' Rights--and Wrongs, n.d.).

Grassroots movements play a crucial role in shaping political agendas and advocating for increased state power. Movements like Occupy Wall Street and Indigenous resistance efforts from Hawaii to the Dakotas have spotlighted the importance of localized action in driving broader political change (What Movements Do to Law, n.d.). The Ferguson and Baltimore protests, spurred by police violence and systemic racism, have also shifted public discourse and policy focus toward state-level reforms in criminal justice. These grassroots initiatives demonstrate how citizens can leverage state power to address specific local issues, potentially bypassing slower federal processes. The growing influence of such movements underscores the enduring relevance of state power in enacting meaningful political change.

However, the push towards increasing state authority is not without risks and challenges. One significant risk involves potential backlash and resistance from federal authorities who may seek to reassert control over critical policy areas. For instance, federal attempts to override state regulations on environmental standards or healthcare provisions could create conflicts and regulatory uncertainty. Additionally, states prioritizing local agendas over national standards might result in a fragmented policy landscape, where disparities in regulations across states could affect national unity and economic stability. There is also the danger of states compromising on citizen rights and freedoms, as seen in historical examples of racial discrimination and voter suppression, suggesting that some states may not always prioritize equitable governance (States' Rights--and Wrongs, n.d.).

Moreover, the resurgence of state power brings about accountability and transparency issues. With states gaining more control, there is a heightened need for robust oversight mechanisms to prevent abuses of power. Examples of legislation reducing oversight, such as laws limiting public access to governmental proceedings or weakening ethics commissions, highlight the potential for increased corruption and diminished public trust. Ensuring that state governments remain transparent and accountable becomes paramount as they undertake more significant responsibilities in governing diverse populations.

The long-term consequences of this shift towards enhanced state power could fundamentally reshape the federalist model in the U.S. As states gain more autonomy and influence, there may be a recalibration of the traditional roles and functions of both state and federal governments. Future legislative battles are likely to revolve around defining the boundaries of state versus federal authority, with implications for governance and policy-making. Understanding these dynamics is crucial for politically active individuals, academics, and activists seeking to navigate and influence the evolving landscape of American federalism.

Chapter 12: Electoral System Overhaul

Revamping the electoral system involves addressing how current practices impact American democracy and civil rights. This chapter delves into the proposed changes under Project 2025, highlighting the potential effects on voter access and participation. By examining historical precedents and modern regulations, we can see patterns that have shaped the country's democratic landscape.

Throughout this chapter, we will explore several key areas: the history and impact of voter ID laws, the consequences of poll taxes and literacy tests, recent legislative changes, and the broader implications of gerrymandering. We'll analyze how these elements collectively influence voter suppression and the erosion of civil rights, offering a critical view of their long-term repercussions on democratic health. The chapter aims to provide a comprehensive look at each factor's role in either hindering or helping create an equitable voting environment.

Voter ID Laws and Voting Rights Restrictions

The implementation of voter ID laws and restrictions on voting rights has significant implications for American democracy, especially concerning the disenfranchisement of marginalized communities. This section analyzes how these laws serve to undermine electoral participation.

First, it's important to understand the historical context of voter ID laws and their discriminatory impact across states. Historically, measures like literacy tests and poll taxes were employed to prevent African Americans from voting. With the civil rights movement, such overt practices were outlawed. However, the emergence of voter ID laws in the modern era can be seen as a continuation of efforts to suppress certain demographics. States began introducing these laws under the guise of protecting electoral integrity, yet their implementation often disproportionately affected low-income and minority voters. According to the Brennan Center for Justice, strict voter ID requirements have been shown to reduce turnout among voters of color significantly (Brennan Center for Justice, 2022).

Moreover, these laws impose unnecessary barriers that disproportionately affect low-income and minority voters. Many people in these demographics lack government-issued IDs due to various socioeconomic factors. For instance, the cost of obtaining an ID, the need to take time off work, and limited access to transportation or vital documents can create substantial hurdles. Research indicates that Black and Latino voters are much less likely to possess the required identification compared to their white counterparts. This effectively denies them their right to vote, further entrenching social inequalities (Hesano, 2023).

Advocates of voter ID laws often frame them as necessary measures to protect against voter fraud. However, evidence suggests that instances of voter impersonation, the type of fraud these laws supposedly prevent, are exceedingly rare. Analysis shows that cases of in-person voter fraud are virtually non-existent when compared to the total number of votes cast. Academic studies have repeatedly demonstrated that other forms of election fraud, such as tampering with absentee ballots, are more common but remain infrequent. The insistence on stringent voter ID laws thus seems disproportionate and misaligned with actual risks, leading critics to conclude that these laws are more about voter suppression than fraud prevention.

Legal challenges against voter ID laws highlight the tension between state regulations and federal voting rights protections. Various lawsuits across the country have sought to overturn these restrictive laws, arguing that they violate the Voting Rights Act by discriminating against minority groups. Court rulings have been mixed; some courts have struck down these laws, while others have upheld them. Notably, the Supreme Court's decision in Shelby County v. Holder (2013) weakened the Voting Rights Act by removing the requirement for certain jurisdictions to obtain federal approval before changing voting laws. This ruling has emboldened several states to pass stricter voter ID requirements without fear of federal intervention.

The legal battles underscore the complex interplay between different levels of government in regulating voting rights. Federal oversight historically ensured that states with histories of discrimination could not enact laws that would disenfranchise minorities. Without this oversight, the responsibility falls on civil rights organizations and individual lawsuits to challenge discriminatory practices. These challenges are resource-intensive and slow, allowing restrictive laws to remain in effect during prolonged legal disputes.

It's also essential to explore contemporary examples to understand the real-world implications of these laws. For instance, North Carolina's voter ID law, which was in place briefly before being struck down, provides a stark example of how such regulations can impact voter turnout. Researchers found a significant drop in the turnout of minority voters who lacked the necessary ID after the law was enacted (Brennan Center for Justice, 2022). Even after the law was repealed, the negative effects on voter participation persisted, revealing the lasting damage caused by these regulations.

Similarly, in Texas, the voter ID law required those without proper identification to sign a “Reasonable Impediments Declaration” to vote. This patchwork solution still created confusion and deterred many eligible voters, particularly Black and Latino individuals, from participating in the electoral process. Studies show that these stopgap measures fail to mitigate the overall suppressive impact of strict voter ID laws (Brennan Center for Justice, 2022).

Ohio's recent legislation restricting the types of acceptable IDs is another example where the political motivations behind these laws come into focus. The new law limits the accepted IDs to a driver’s license, state identification card, passport, or military identification. Critics argue that this change disproportionately affects marginalized groups, including young voters, the elderly, and low-income individuals who are less likely to possess these forms of identification. Legal challenges against this restriction highlight its potential to disenfranchise thousands of voters, with plaintiffs arguing that it places an undue burden on specific demographic groups (Hesano, 2023).

The broader implications of these restrictive measures extend beyond individual states, affecting the overall health of American democracy. By creating barriers to voting, these laws contribute to lower electoral participation rates among already marginalized communities, exacerbating existing inequalities. In turn, this impacts the representative nature of elected bodies, skewing policies away from the interests of all constituents and towards the preferences of a more selectively enfranchised electorate.

Voter ID laws and voting restrictions reflect deeper systemic issues within the American electoral system. They reveal ongoing struggles over who gets to participate fully in democratic processes and how power is distributed across racial and socioeconomic lines. Addressing these issues requires comprehensive reforms aimed at making voting more accessible, such as automatic voter registration, expanded early voting, and easier access to mail-in ballots.

Effects of Poll Taxes and Literacy Tests

In examining the progressive landscape of electoral reform, it becomes essential to draw parallels between modern voting restrictions and historical barriers to voting. Historically, practices like poll taxes and literacy tests were designed explicitly to suppress minority voting. These methods of disenfranchisement were not just about blocking access to the ballot box; they were indicators of broader systemic racism that sought to maintain white supremacy by excluding Black citizens and other minorities from democratic participation.

Contemporary voting laws, although more covert in their intentions, often serve similar purposes. For instance, voter purges, such as those upheld by the Supreme Court in its Husted v. A. Philip Randolph Institute decision, have resulted in the removal of millions of eligible Americans of color from voter rolls (Solomon et al., 2019). Ohio's purge of 846,000 disproportionately Black voters is reminiscent of past poll tax efforts—designed to reduce political power among marginalized communities. Although these modern strategies are framed as maintaining the integrity of voter rolls, their disproportionate impact on Black voters illustrates an ongoing legacy of systemic racism in voting regulations.

To further understand the persistence of such measures, it helps to consider the 24th Amendment, which banned poll taxes. Yet, modern iterations of these taxes have surfaced, as seen in Florida's financial restrictions imposed on former felons seeking to restore their voting rights. After Florida voters overwhelmingly supported a change to the state constitution to restore these rights, lawmakers countered with regulations that disproportionately affected Black residents (Solomon et al., 2019). This reflects a clear parallel to historical poll taxes and underscores the persistence of discriminatory tactics.

By comparing these contemporary measures with historical practices, it is evident that both aim to undermine democratic participation by minorities. These modern restrictions not only highlight systemic racism but also threaten the democratic processes built on inclusivity and representation. Democracy is fundamentally predicated on the equal participation of all citizens. However, when certain groups are systematically excluded through legislation, the foundational principles of democracy are eroded.

The need for vigilance in safeguarding voting rights cannot be overstated. Just as past generations fought against poll taxes and literacy tests, contemporary advocates must remain alert to new forms of suppression. The rollback of provisions like those in the Voting Rights Act, particularly following the Shelby County v. Holder decision, has led to a surge in state-level voter suppression laws that disproportionately impact voters of color (ACLU, 2023). These include stringent voter ID laws, cuts to early voting, and arbitrary restrictions on absentee voting, which collectively contribute to disenfranchisement and weakened electoral participation.

Drawing on historical examples can vividly illustrate why current measures should be scrutinized and challenged. During the Jim Crow era, barriers such as literacy tests were ostensibly neutral criteria applied to all potential voters. However, in practice, they were almost exclusively used to disenfranchise Black voters. In the same vein, today's voter ID laws are touted as necessary safeguards against fraud, yet studies consistently show that voter impersonation is extremely rare. Instead, these laws create hurdles for low-income and minority voters who may lack the requisite identification.

Moreover, recent legislative efforts to reintroduce preclearance requirements under the John R. Lewis Voting Rights Advancement Act underscore the critical importance of federal oversight in preventing discriminatory voting practices. Had the Supreme Court not gutted the VRA a decade ago, many voters in jurisdictions with histories of voting discrimination would still enjoy protections against racially motivated changes to voting laws (ACLU, 2023). Reinstating these protections is vital to ensuring that future generations do not face the same barriers as their predecessors.

The argument that such tactics threaten the integrity of democratic processes is compelling. Democracy thrives on inclusivity and broad representation. When laws and practices systematically exclude certain demographics, the resulting government does not fully represent the will of the people. This undermines public trust in democratic institutions and weakens the overall health of the political system. Voter suppression tactics, whether overt or covert, compromise the principles upon which American democracy is founded.

It is also important to acknowledge the broader implications of these measures. Systemic voter suppression contributes to racial inequality, perpetuating a cycle where marginalized communities remain underrepresented and underserved. As demographic shifts continue to diversify the electorate, there is a pressing need to ensure that all voices are heard and valued. This involves not only resisting attempts to roll back voting rights but also actively working to expand access and participation.

Illustrating the need for vigilance in safeguarding voting rights, one can look at the various grassroots movements and advocacy efforts currently underway. Organizations across the country are mobilizing to educate voters, challenge restrictive laws in court, and push for comprehensive reforms that protect and enhance the right to vote. These efforts are crucial in countering the resurgence of voter suppression and ensuring that every citizen can participate equally in the democratic process.

Reflecting on past and present challenges reveals the enduring struggle for equitable voting rights in America. While significant progress has been made over the decades, the persistence of discriminatory practices highlights the need for continued vigilance and activism. By drawing parallels between historical and modern barriers to voting, we gain a clearer understanding of the systematic efforts to disenfranchise minority voters and the imperative to safeguard our democracy against such threats.

Case Studies of Recent Legislative Changes

Stringent voter ID laws have been a contentious issue in several states, with significant implications for American democracy and civil rights. This subpoint examines the impact of these laws in various states, analyzing their consequences on voter turnout, community responses to counteract disenfranchisement, political motivations behind such legislation, and potential cybersecurity risks related to digital voting tools.

The implementation of stringent voter ID laws has been particularly evident in states like Georgia, Texas, and Wisconsin. These states have adopted rigorous identification requirements that critics argue disproportionately affect certain demographics, notably low-income individuals, minorities, the elderly, and people with disabilities. Evidence suggests that these laws contribute to a decrease in voter turnout among these groups. For instance, studies indicate that the introduction of strict voter ID laws in Texas led to a noticeable decline in turnout among Black and Latino voters, groups less likely to possess the required forms of identification (Root & Ives-Rublee, 2021).

This reduction in voter turnout is not just a statistical anomaly but a reflection of broader democratic challenges. The disenfranchisement of these communities raises serious questions about the inclusivity and fairness of the electoral system. It perpetuates a cycle where marginalized groups become even more excluded from the political process, thus weakening their ability to influence policy decisions that directly affect their lives.

Community responses to stringent voter ID laws have been varied and robust. Activists and organization coalitions have mobilized to mitigate the adverse effects of these regulations. For example, grassroots movements in states with harsh ID laws have focused on voter education campaigns, helping citizens understand new requirements and assisting them in obtaining the necessary documentation. In Georgia, community leaders launched initiatives providing transportation to government offices where voters could secure acceptable IDs.

Additionally, legal battles have played a crucial role in addressing these legislative measures. Organizations such as the American Civil Liberties Union (ACLU) and the Brennan Center for Justice frequently challenge voter ID laws in court, arguing that they infringe upon constitutional voting rights. Through these efforts, some voter ID laws have been blocked or softened, yet many remain in force, continuing to pose hurdles for sizable voter segments.

Moreover, community responses have highlighted the importance of organizing at the grassroots level to ensure voter protection and engagement. Local advocacy groups often partner with national organizations to create comprehensive strategies that address both immediate and long-term needs. These partnerships enable the pooling of resources and expertise, fostering a more resilient response against disenfranchising policies.

The political motivations behind the push for stringent voter ID laws are multifaceted and complex. Proponents argue that such measures are essential to preventing voter fraud and ensuring electoral integrity. However, empirical evidence suggests that instances of voter impersonation fraud are extremely rare. Instead, the push for more restrictive voting laws often coincides with demographic shifts that threaten the political dominance of established power structures (Ian Vandewalker, 2020). As the electorate becomes increasingly diverse, some lawmakers may see voter ID laws as a tool to preserve their electoral advantage by curbing the participation of minority and marginalized voters who are perceived as less likely to support their agendas.

This strategic calculus underscores the broader dynamics of power and control within American politics. By imposing barriers to voting, legislators can shape the electorate in ways that maintain their grip on power, even as society evolves. This manipulation of the democratic process not only undermines the principle of equal representation but also erodes public trust in the electoral system.

In addition to the socio-political implications, the rise of digital voting tools introduces cybersecurity concerns that could further complicate the landscape of electoral integrity. While technological advancements offer the promise of greater accessibility and efficiency, they also present new vulnerabilities that malicious actors could exploit. Cyber threats, including hacking and misinformation campaigns, pose significant risks to the reliability of digital voting systems. For instance, during the 2020 elections, there were reports of cyber-attacks targeting voter databases and election infrastructure, highlighting the need for robust cybersecurity measures (Ian Vandewalker, 2020).

These security challenges necessitate a proactive approach to protect digital voting tools. Election officials must invest in advanced cybersecurity protocols to safeguard the integrity of electronic voting systems. This includes regular audits, vulnerability assessments, and the implementation of best practices recommended by cybersecurity experts. Furthermore, transparent communication with the public about these measures is vital to maintaining confidence in the electoral process.

Given the critical nature of this issue, it is imperative to develop comprehensive strategies that address both the technical and human elements of cybersecurity. Training programs for election staff, collaborations with tech companies, and federal support for state and local election security initiatives are essential components of a holistic approach to securing digital voting tools.

Understanding Gerrymandering and Its Consequences

Redistricting and gerrymandering are pivotal yet contentious aspects of the electoral system. As states redraw their electoral districts once every decade, this process can significantly influence electoral outcomes and contribute to political polarization. Gerrymandering, the manipulation of district boundaries to favor one party over another, has a long history and far-reaching consequences. This section delves into what gerrymandering entails, its historical evolution, how it leads to uncompetitive elections, recent legal attempts to curb it, and successful case studies where reforms have been implemented.

Gerrymandering is the practice of manipulating electoral district boundaries to create an unfair political advantage. Originating in the early 19th century, the term gerrymandering comes from Elbridge Gerry, a Massachusetts governor who signed a bill that redistricted the state to benefit his party. Over time, gerrymandering has evolved, especially with advancements in technology that allow for highly precise manipulation of district lines. The core techniques involve "cracking" and "packing." Cracking splits a voting bloc across several districts to dilute their voting power, while packing concentrates voters of one type into a single district to reduce their influence in other areas.

The implications of gerrymandering on democracy are profound. When politicians manipulate district boundaries to entrench their power, it often results in uncompetitive elections. By making certain districts overwhelmingly favor one party, gerrymandering diminishes competition, as incumbents face little risk of losing their seats. This lack of competition discourages voter engagement and participation. When electoral outcomes become predictable, voters may feel that their votes don't matter, leading to apathy and reduced turnout. In extreme cases, gerrymandering can disenfranchise entire communities, particularly those of color, by diluting their collective voting strength.

Recent court rulings and legislative efforts have sought to address the adverse effects of gerrymandering. However, these attempts have met with mixed success. In 2019, the Supreme Court ruled in Rucho v. Common Cause that partisan gerrymandering claims present political questions beyond the reach of federal courts. This decision effectively left the regulation of gerrymandering to state courts and legislatures. Some states have responded by passing laws to create independent redistricting commissions aimed at drawing fairer maps. For example, California's independent commission has been lauded for creating more balanced districts that better reflect the state's diverse population. Similarly, Michigan voters approved a ballot initiative in 2018 to establish an independent commission, removing redistricting power from the legislature.

Despite these strides, substantial challenges remain. Legislative bodies that maintain control over redistricting often continue to draw lines that favor incumbents or the dominant party in the state. Such practices perpetuate a cycle of political polarization, as elected officials cater to increasingly partisan constituencies, further deepening the divide between opposing parties. A significant portion of this polarization stems from the strategic use of data and sophisticated mapping software. These tools enable politicians to predict voting patterns with remarkable accuracy, allowing them to craft districts that maximize political advantage.

Several states offer models of how to navigate and rectify the issue of gerrymandering successfully. Arizona, for instance, established an Independent Redistricting Commission following a voter-approved initiative in 2000. This commission uses set criteria to ensure that districts are competitive and representative. As a result, Arizona has seen more equitable and competitive elections. Another notable example is Iowa, where a nonpartisan legislative agency draws the district maps which the state legislature then approves. This method has fostered a more transparent and fair redistricting process, contributing to greater public trust in the electoral system.

The impact of gerrymandering also extends to policy outcomes within legislative bodies. When districts are drawn to secure safe seats for incumbents, representatives may become less responsive to the needs and preferences of their constituents, knowing that their re-election is almost guaranteed. This dynamic can lead to extreme partisanship and gridlock, as legislators prioritize party loyalty over bipartisan cooperation. Consequently, policies that could benefit a broader segment of the population often stall or fail to materialize, exacerbating public disillusionment with the political process.

Chapter 13: Corporate Influence in Politics

Corporate influence in politics is a complex and multi-layered phenomenon that impacts governance, policy-making, and democracy. By leveraging resources such as lobbying and campaign contributions, corporations can shape legislation and regulatory practices to align with their interests. This influence has raised critical concerns about the balance of power between corporate entities and democratic institutions, highlighting issues of transparency, accountability, and public trust. The entanglement of corporate agendas with political decision-making can fundamentally alter the landscape of governance, often prioritizing profit over public welfare. Understanding these dynamics is crucial for those aiming to protect democratic values and advocate for fair policies.

This chapter delves into several key components to illustrate how corporate clout shapes the policies outlined in Project 2025. It begins by dissecting the mechanics of lobbying, providing a detailed look at how corporations engage directly with lawmakers to influence policy. Following this, it examines the impact of dark money on elections and governance, shedding light on the lack of transparency in political funding. Several case studies are presented to offer concrete examples of corporate influence in action, demonstrating how specific industries have successfully swayed regulations and laws to their advantage. Lastly, the chapter explores regulatory capture, where industries exert substantial control over the agencies meant to regulate them, leading to policies that often favor business interests over the public good. This comprehensive analysis aims to equip readers with a nuanced understanding of the profound ways in which corporate interests shape modern politics.

Lobbying and Campaign Contributions

Corporate lobbying and campaign contributions are powerful tools that corporations use to influence political decisions, thus reinforcing the architecture of policies outlined in Project 2025. This subpoint unravels the mechanics of lobbying, the impact of dark money, case studies demonstrating corporate influence, and the phenomenon of regulatory capture.

The Mechanics of Lobbying

Lobbying is a key mechanism through which corporations attempt to sway political outcomes. In the U.S., lobbying involves direct interaction with lawmakers and government officials to advocate for policies beneficial to the corporation's interests. Lobbyists, often hired from prestigious firms or as former politicians themselves, leverage their connections and knowledge of the legislative process to push agendas that align with corporate goals. They craft detailed policy proposals, provide expert testimony in legislative hearings, and engage in informal discussions with legislators. The goal is to shape legislation in ways that favor corporate interests, which can include anything from tax breaks to the deregulation of certain industries.

Moreover, lobbyists not only work to promote new policies but also defend existing regulations that benefit their clients. By building relationships with key decision-makers, they gain early access to information about upcoming legislative processes and can influence the content and direction of bills before they even reach public debate stages.

Impact of Dark Money

Dark money refers to anonymous political donations that obscure the true source of funding. These contributions are often funneled through nonprofit organizations that are not required to disclose their donors, leading to significant amounts of money influencing elections without transparency. According to Kennedy & Root (2017), more than $800 million has been spent by dark money groups since 2010, significantly impacting U.S. elections.

The lack of transparency in these contributions undermines democratic accountability and allows wealthy individuals or corporations to have a disproportionate influence on the political process. For instance, during Betsy DeVos's confirmation for Secretary of Education, dark money groups spent heavily on ad campaigns supporting her nomination. Without knowing who funds such efforts, voters cannot fully understand the motivations behind certain political endorsements or opposition.

Case Studies of Corporate Influence

One vivid example of corporate influence related to Project 2025 can be seen in the financial sector. During Trump's presidency, several actions were taken that aligned closely with the interests of financial corporations. Laws like the rollback of Dodd-Frank regulations exemplify how lobbying efforts shaped policy. These regulatory changes were heavily lobbied for by financial institutions seeking to reduce oversight and increase profitability.

Similarly, in the educational sector, Robert Eitel, who worked for Bridgepoint Education, was appointed to the Department of Education while still connected to his former employer. The department subsequently delayed parts of the Gainful Employment Rule, which was designed to protect students from being misled by for-profit colleges (Kennedy & Root, 2017). This case illustrates how close ties between regulators and the industries they are supposed to oversee can result in policies that favor corporate interests at the expense of consumer protection.

Regulatory Capture

Regulatory capture occurs when industry stakeholders exert overwhelming influence over the agencies meant to regulate them, often resulting in favorable policies that undermine the agency's original mission. For instance, the Environmental Protection Agency (EPA) under Project 2025 might be influenced by fossil fuel companies to relax environmental regulations, thereby prioritizing economic gains over environmental protection.

This phenomenon is not new. Historically, industries such as pharmaceuticals, finance, and energy have successfully captured their respective regulatory agencies by ensuring that former industry executives are placed in key governmental positions. This practice blurs the line between regulation and business interests, making it difficult for agencies to enforce rules that could harm the profits of the industries they are supposed to regulate.

To combat regulatory capture, stronger ethics rules and transparency measures are essential. For example, waivers allowing former industry lobbyists to bypass ethics requirements should be made publicly available, ensuring that conflicts of interest are identified and mitigated (Kennedy & Root, 2017).

The Mechanics of Lobbying

Lobbying in the U.S. political system is a multifaceted mechanism, intricately woven into the fabric of governance and democracy. At its core, lobbying involves individuals or groups attempting to influence political decisions by engaging with lawmakers, regulators, and other decision-makers. This process is legalized through strict regulations, but the dynamics of lobbying present several critical challenges to democratic representation and governance.

One fundamental issue is that lobbying often skews policy toward corporate interests, undermining democratic representation. Corporations wield significant economic power, enabling them to hire professional lobbyists who have the expertise and political connections necessary to influence legislation. These lobbyists provide policymakers with information, draft legislative proposals, and advocate for policies that align with their employers' interests. The result is a political landscape where corporate agendas frequently take precedence over the needs and voices of ordinary citizens.

Corporations employ lobbyists to access decision-makers, effectively prioritizing wealth over public needs. The lobbyists are often former politicians or government officials, leveraging their personal relationships and insider knowledge. This revolving door between the private sector and government creates a symbiotic relationship where corporate priorities are seamlessly integrated into the legislative process. The ability to engage directly with legislators gives corporations a distinct advantage, allowing them to shape policies to their benefit while marginalizing less affluent stakeholders.

The legislative outcomes, therefore, frequently reflect corporate agendas rather than constituents' interests. Policies resulting from this influence are typically designed to enhance corporate profitability, sometimes at the expense of public welfare. For instance, tax reforms may disproportionately favor large corporations, environmental regulations might be weakened to benefit industrial polluters, and health care policies could be altered to suit pharmaceutical giants. Such outcomes can exacerbate social inequality, hinder environmental protection, and restrict access to essential services.

Specific examples illustrate how corporate entities have succeeded in shaping pertinent legislation. One notable case involves the pharmaceutical industry. In 2003, the Medicare Prescription Drug, Improvement, and Modernization Act was passed, which included a provision prohibiting Medicare from negotiating drug prices. This legislation, heavily influenced by pharmaceutical lobbyists, led to significantly higher costs for prescription drugs under Medicare, benefiting drug manufacturers while placing a financial burden on taxpayers and seniors. Another example is the deregulation of the financial industry in the late 1990s, culminating in the repeal of the Glass-Steagall Act. Banks and financial institutions lobbied intensively for this change, arguing it was necessary for their competitiveness. However, the subsequent lack of regulation contributed to the 2008 financial crisis, underscoring the detrimental impact of corporate lobbying on economic stability.

These examples highlight the broader issue of regulatory capture, where industries exert undue influence over the agencies meant to regulate them. When regulators are swayed by the sectors they oversee, policies tend to become more accommodating to business interests, potentially compromising public safety and welfare. The Environmental Protection Agency (EPA), for instance, has faced criticism for being influenced by the industries it regulates, leading to weaker enforcement of environmental laws and standards.

Impact of Dark Money

Anonymous campaign contributions, also known as dark money, play a significant role in the political landscape. These contributions often come from organizations designed to obscure the sources of funding, thus reducing accountability and transparency within the democratic process. One of the main issues with dark money organizations is their ability to operate without disclosing their donors. For instance, politically active nonprofits such as 501(c)(4)s are not legally required to disclose their donors even if they spend to influence elections (*Dark Money Basics, 2016*). This loophole allows substantial sums of money to pour into political campaigns without public knowledge of who is behind these contributions.

The lack of transparency in campaign financing has profound implications for democracy. When wealthy individuals or corporations can donate large sums anonymously, they can exert a disproportionate influence on election outcomes and subsequent policymaking. This creates an imbalance where the interests of the few overshadow the needs of the many, distorting democratic processes. The Citizens United v. FEC Supreme Court ruling in 2010 significantly contributed to this issue by allowing unlimited contributions from corporations and unions to super PACs (*5 Ways Secret Money Makes Its Way into Our Elections*, 2022). Super PACs, although required to disclose their donors, can still receive funds from dark money groups, effectively masking the true source of their financial power.

As a result of these practices, voter trust in political institutions diminishes. When citizens perceive that elections can be bought by anonymous, wealthy contributors, they may feel that their votes carry less weight. This perceived corruption can lead to disillusionment and apathy, undermining the very foundation of democratic engagement. The influx of dark money erodes the principle of one person, one vote, replacing it with a system where finances might dictate political outcomes. An example of this is the rise of "pop-up" super PACs that emerge just before elections and delay donor disclosure until after votes have been cast (*5 Ways Secret Money Makes Its Way into Our Elections*, 2022). Such tactics further obscure accountability and undermine voters' ability to make informed choices.

Moreover, these anonymous contributions often bypass traditional democratic processes. By funneling money through opaque networks and shell companies, donors can delegate power to corporate entities without direct public scrutiny. This form of influence allows corporations to shape policy and governance in ways that serve their interests rather than the public good. A network of 501(c)(4) organizations can act as intermediaries, channeling funds to super PACs while concealing the original donors (*5 Ways Secret Money Makes Its Way into Our Elections*, 2022). Consequently, policies and legislation may reflect corporate priorities instead of addressing the broader populace's needs.

To illustrate, consider the case of healthcare reform. Dark money can be used to fund extensive advertising campaigns promoting specific legislative agendas favored by corporate donors. These advertisements, often framed as grassroots movements, can sway public opinion and pressure lawmakers to support policies that benefit the funding corporations. Meanwhile, the general public remains unaware of the financial motivations underlying these campaigns, believing them to be genuine expressions of public interest. This manipulation of democratic discourse highlights the detrimental impact of dark money on policy formation and governance.

In addition, dark money's influence extends to environmental regulations. Corporations with vested interests in maintaining lax environmental standards can use anonymous contributions to lobby against stricter regulations. By funding politicians and advocacy groups that oppose environmental protections, these corporations can ensure that their business operations remain unimpeded. This dynamic not only harms the environment but also subverts the will of the electorate, who may overwhelmingly support stronger environmental safeguards.

The entanglement of dark money and politics underscores the need for greater transparency in campaign finance. Without transparency, the potential for abuse and corruption remains high. Reforms aimed at increasing disclosure requirements for all political donations would help restore accountability and build public trust in the electoral process. For instance, eliminating the anonymity provided to 501(c)(4) organizations and requiring full disclosure of all political contributions would be a step toward ensuring that voters have access to information about who is influencing their representatives.

Furthermore, enforcing existing campaign finance laws more rigorously could deter the use of straw donor schemes and other illicit methods of funneling secret money into politics. Stricter oversight by the Federal Election Commission (FEC) and greater penalties for violations could mitigate the pervasive influence of dark money. It is essential for democratic integrity that the origins of political contributions be transparent, preventing the undue influence of hidden donors.

Public-Private Partnerships and Their Implications

The proliferation of public-private partnerships (PPPs) within Project 2025 demands critical evaluation due to their profound implications for democracy and citizen rights. These partnerships, while often touted as innovative solutions to social issues, can sometimes prioritize corporate profit over the public interest.

Public-private partnerships are frequently framed as efficient means to address societal challenges. Governments partner with private entities to leverage resources, technology, and expertise that might otherwise be unavailable through public funding alone. This approach ostensibly benefits society by addressing needs in areas such as infrastructure, healthcare, and education. However, the inherent profit motivation of private companies means that public interests can often be overshadowed by the desire for financial gain. This misalignment between public good and private profit may lead to decisions that do not necessarily align with community needs or broader societal benefits.

Examples from various sectors illustrate how corporations can drive public agendas rather than meeting community needs. Consider the privatization of water services in several municipalities. While the initial goal was to improve water distribution and quality, numerous cases reveal that the primary focus shifted toward maximizing profits. Issues like increased water rates and reduced maintenance investments emerged, adversely affecting residents. Similarly, in healthcare, PPPs aimed at building hospitals or providing medical services have sometimes led to higher costs for patients and a concentration on profitable treatments rather than necessary, less lucrative, preventive care.

Another concerning aspect of PPPs is the restrictions they impose within privatized programs, which can systematically exclude marginalized groups. For instance, when transportation systems are privatized, fare increases and route reductions often disproportionately impact low-income individuals who rely on affordable and accessible public transport. In the educational sector, privately managed charter schools may cater predominantly to students from more affluent families, thereby deepening existing inequalities in the education system. The systematic exclusion of marginalized communities from essential services exacerbates social inequities and undermines the core democratic principle of equal access to public goods.

To mitigate the risks associated with PPPs, robust governance frameworks and accountability measures are essential. Ensuring transparency in the formation and execution of these partnerships can help safeguard against conflicts of interest and ensure that public welfare remains the primary focus. Accountability mechanisms, such as independent audits and public reporting requirements, are vital to monitor the performance of PPPs and ensure that they meet agreed-upon standards and social objectives. Additionally, incorporating community input into decision-making processes can help tailor PPP projects to better reflect the actual needs and priorities of the affected populations.

Effective oversight is crucial in preventing abuses and ensuring that PPPs do not become vehicles for unchecked corporate influence. Regulatory bodies must be empowered to enforce compliance with contractual obligations and penalize deviations that harm public interests. Moreover, there should be clear provisions for renegotiating or terminating partnerships if they fail to deliver promised benefits or if they exacerbate social inequalities.

In examining the PPP model within the context of Project 2025, it becomes evident that while these partnerships have potential benefits, their implementation must be carefully scrutinized to avoid detrimental effects on democracy and citizen rights. The privatization trend, driven by the assumption that private entities inherently operate more efficiently and effectively, overlooks the nuanced impacts on public welfare and social equity. A balance must be struck where the efficiency and innovation of the private sector can be harnessed without compromising the fundamental responsibilities of the government to serve and protect its citizens.

By critically assessing the real-world outcomes of PPPs, policymakers can develop more nuanced approaches that integrate accountability and equity considerations. Only through such comprehensive evaluation can PPPs truly serve the public interest and contribute to the sustainable and equitable development envisioned in overarching policy frameworks like Project 2025.

Chapter 14: Impact on Minority Communities

Assessing the impacts of Project 2025 on minority communities reveals critical concerns about exacerbating existing disparities and undermining hard-won rights. The policies proposed under this project, including tax cuts and deregulations, raise alarms over their potential to widen income gaps and deepen socio-economic divides. This chapter delves into the complexities of how these fiscal measures may disproportionately affect racial and ethnic minorities, who historically face significant economic disadvantages. By examining real-life examples and historical precedents, it uncovers how seemingly neutral policies can perpetuate cycles of poverty and inequality.

In addition to economic impacts, the chapter explores the potential consequences for healthcare access and public health within marginalized communities. With proposed funding cuts for essential services, minority populations could see a deterioration in health outcomes, further entrenching systemic inequities. Educational policy changes are analyzed to understand their effect on minority students' opportunities, while increased law enforcement measures are scrutinized for their likelihood of straining relationships between police and minority communities. Finally, by evaluating these multifaceted issues, the chapter aims to provide a comprehensive understanding of the stakes involved and encourage proactive strategies for advocacy and resistance.

Racial and Ethnic Disparities in Policy Impacts

Project 2025's policies have significant implications for racial and ethnic minority communities, exacerbating existing systemic inequities. The proposed tax cuts and deregulations in Project 2025 are likely to widen income gaps between white and minority populations. Historically, affluent whites tend to benefit more from such fiscal policies due to their existing financial stability and access to resources. Conversely, minority communities often find themselves disadvantaged as they lack the same level of economic security. This disparity is not merely theoretical; it reflects the ongoing struggles faced by minority groups who already encounter significant economic disadvantages.

One key example can be seen in regions where similar policies have led to prolonged poverty cycles among minority groups. For instance, deregulation measures in certain states have historically resulted in job losses and reduced wages for low-income workers, disproportionately affecting communities of color. These trends highlight how fiscal policies that ostensibly promote economic growth can, in practice, deepen racial and economic divides.

Reduced funding for healthcare services under Project 2025 presents another critical issue. Minority communities already suffer from higher rates of chronic illnesses and limited access to quality healthcare. Data shows that these communities experience worse health outcomes and higher mortality rates compared to their white counterparts. The potential cuts in healthcare funding could exacerbate these issues, leading to further disparities in public health. As healthcare facilities close or reduce services due to lack of funding, marginalized populations may find it increasingly difficult to receive necessary treatments, further deteriorating their health status.

Moreover, cuts in healthcare funding can lead to reductions in preventive care, which is crucial for managing and mitigating long-term health issues prevalent in minority communities. Without sufficient access to preventive services, conditions such as diabetes, hypertension, and asthma—already more common in these communities—are likely to worsen, thereby increasing healthcare costs in the long run.

Educational policy changes proposed by Project 2025 also pose a considerable threat to minority students' opportunities. Funding cuts in education could result in larger class sizes, fewer resources, and diminished support for students in marginalized communities. Such changes undermine the quality of education and limit the chances for minority students to succeed academically. Larger class sizes mean less individual attention for students, while fewer resources can result in outdated materials and inadequate facilities.

A historical perspective shows the detrimental effects of educational resource reductions on minority student performance. For example, during previous periods of educational budget cuts, schools in predominantly Black and Brown communities struggled considerably, with declining graduation rates and lower college admission numbers. These precedents underscore the vital need for sustained educational investment to ensure fair opportunities for all students, regardless of their racial or socio-economic background.

Additionally, harsher law enforcement measures enabled by Project 2025 may increase instances of racial profiling and strain relationships between minority communities and police forces. The emphasis on stringent policing strategies has historically resulted in disproportionate targeting and arrest rates among racial minorities. These practices not only perpetuate a climate of fear but also erode trust in law enforcement agencies, making community-police collaboration difficult.

Increased law enforcement measures often lead to higher incarceration rates for minor offenses, particularly in neighborhoods with larger minority populations. This phenomenon, known as "over-policing," serves to further entrench systemic biases within the criminal justice system. Minority individuals are more likely to face arrests, convictions, and harsher sentences compared to their white counterparts for similar offenses.

The impact of strained police-community relations cannot be overstated. It impedes effective policing and public safety, as community members become hesitant to report crimes or cooperate with investigations. Building trust between law enforcement and minority communities requires reforms that emphasize transparency, accountability, and equitable treatment under the law.

Unfortunately, the proposed measures in Project 2025 seem poised to move in the opposite direction.

Effect on LGBTQ+ Rights and Protections

Evaluating the Potential Threats to LGBTQ+ Rights and Protections Under Project 2025

Project 2025 poses significant threats to the rights and protections of LGBTQ+ individuals across various aspects of their lives. The potential rollback of legal safeguards is alarming, particularly in the employment and housing sectors.

Proposed laws under Project 2025 could significantly undermine existing protections for LGBTQ+ individuals, especially in employment and housing. Currently, federal laws prevent discrimination based on sexual orientation and gender identity. However, Project 2025 aims to dismantle these crucial protections. Without these safeguards, LGBTQ+ individuals may face heightened discrimination, limiting their opportunities in the workforce and housing markets. Employers and landlords might feel emboldened to discriminate without fear of legal repercussions, exacerbating economic and social marginalization for many within the LGBTQ+ community.

Changes in healthcare policies proposed by Project 2025 are another area of concern. These changes could drastically reduce access to gender-affirming care, which is vital for the well-being of transgender individuals. Gender-affirming care includes medical procedures and treatments that align individuals' physical appearances with their gender identities, significantly improving their mental health and overall quality of life. With reduced support for such care, transgender individuals may encounter significant barriers when seeking necessary medical treatments. This can lead to increased rates of anxiety, depression, and other mental health issues among LGBTQ+ populations. Furthermore, limited access to affirming healthcare can result in severe physical health consequences for those who cannot obtain appropriate medical treatments.

Educational settings also come under threat from Project 2025, with reductions in support systems likely to increase risks of bullying and harassment for LGBTQ+ youth. Schools have made strides in creating inclusive environments through anti-bullying policies and supportive resources for LGBTQ+ students. However, Project 2025's approach may strip away these essential protections, leaving vulnerable students exposed to higher levels of victimization. Bullying and harassment can have long-lasting detrimental effects on the mental health and academic performance of LGBTQ+ students, leading to higher dropout rates and diminished educational achievements. The lack of supportive environments can perpetuate a cycle of exclusion and hinder the personal development of young LGBTQ+ individuals.

Despite these looming threats, there is potential for increased mobilization and activism within LGBTQ+ communities as a countermeasure. Historically, grassroots movements have played a pivotal role in advancing LGBTQ+ rights and challenging discriminatory practices. For instance, the Stonewall Riots of 1969 marked a turning point for LGBTQ+ activism, sparking a nationwide movement for equal rights. In response to Project 2025, we may see a resurgence of similar grassroots efforts aimed at protecting hard-won rights and advocating for more inclusive policies. Community organizing, advocacy, and public demonstrations could become more prevalent as LGBTQ+ individuals and allies unite to resist regressive measures.

The erosion of legal protections would not only affect LGBTQ+ individuals' day-to-day lives but also signal a broader societal regression. It undermines progress made over decades and sets a dangerous precedent for the treatment of other marginalized groups. As history has shown, attacks on one group's rights can quickly lead to wider social injustices affecting multiple communities. Therefore, politically active individuals, academics, and activists must remain vigilant and proactive in defending LGBTQ+ rights.

The implications of Project 2025 extend beyond individual hardships, potentially influencing the national discourse on equality and justice. The removal of LGBTQ-inclusive language from federal agencies is indicative of a broader agenda to erase the visibility and recognition of diverse identities. Such actions could foster a culture of intolerance, making it increasingly difficult for LGBTQ+ individuals to live openly and authentically. This erasure extends to critical areas like diversity and inclusion programs, which play a vital role in fostering acceptance and understanding across different sectors of society.

Economic Inequality Among Minorities

The economic consequences of Project 2025 on minority communities are profound and multifaceted, emphasizing the widening wealth disparities that have long plagued marginalized groups. Historically marginalized populations, particularly African Americans and Hispanics, already grapple with significant economic disadvantages. Data illustrates a stark contrast in median household incomes and overall wealth between these communities and their white counterparts. For instance, African American families typically have substantially lower household incomes—around $45,870—nearly 40% less than white households (Steele, 2022). The wealth gap is even more pronounced, with white families averaging six times more wealth than Black families.

New tax and deregulation policies proposed under Project 2025 threaten to exacerbate these existing disparities. These measures often result in greater benefits for wealthier segments of society, primarily affluent whites, while perpetuating cycles of poverty for minority communities. Lowering tax rates for the highest income brackets means less revenue for public programs that assist those with fewer resources. Historical patterns support this concern. For example, the tax cuts implemented during the Reagan administration disproportionately benefited the wealthy and resulted in reduced funding for social services that minority communities relied upon (Schermerhorn, 2023).

The historical context further underscores the potential negative impact of such policies. During the Clinton and Bush administrations, deregulatory measures and tax cuts similarly contributed to widening income gaps. For instance, Clinton-era policies, including the repeal of the Glass-Steagall Act, laid the groundwork for the 2008 housing crisis, which saw Black households lose nearly half of their wealth compared to just over a quarter for white households. George W. Bush's continuation of these deregulatory practices and extension of subprime loans to Black homeowners regardless of income exacerbated the financial collapse's effects on minority populations (Schermerhorn, 2023).

Moreover, Project 2025's emphasis on deregulation could lead to further economic instability for minority communities. Deregulation has historically led to environments where financial and economic protections are weakened, making it harder for low-income families to build and sustain wealth. The reduction of regulatory oversight typically favors large corporations and wealthy individuals, leaving small businesses and lower-income workers vulnerable to economic shifts and exploitation.

To address these widening disparities, the necessity of equitable economic policies becomes apparent. Policies must be designed to provide support and opportunities specifically targeted at lifting minority communities out of poverty. This includes comprehensive tax reforms that shift the burden away from the working class and onto higher-income earners, as well as increased investment in social programs that directly benefit marginalized groups.

Equitable economic policies should also focus on expanding access to education, healthcare, and housing. Investment in quality education for minority students, coupled with policies that ensure affordable housing and accessible healthcare, can provide the foundation for economic advancement. Additionally, enforcing fair labor practices and ensuring equal pay can help mitigate some of the economic challenges faced by minority communities.

Past efforts to implement such policies show mixed results but offer valuable lessons. The Affordable Care Act, for instance, significantly expanded healthcare coverage among minorities, suggesting that targeted policy interventions can yield positive outcomes. However, the persistence of the racial wealth gap indicates that more aggressive and comprehensive measures are required.

Public opinion also supports more progressive tax policies aimed at reducing inequality. There is significant support for proposals to raise top tax rates and close loopholes that allow the wealthy to avoid paying their fair share. By adopting policies that redistribute wealth more equitably and investing in programs that benefit lower-income communities, policymakers can begin to address the systemic issues that contribute to economic disparities.

Finally, equitable economic policies must be part of a broader strategy to dismantle systemic racism. Economic reforms alone cannot eliminate the deeply entrenched racial biases that affect employment, wages, and access to resources. Therefore, any economic policy aiming to reduce wealth disparities must also include components that address racial discrimination in all its forms.

Healthcare Access and Public Health

Focusing on the critical impact of reduced funding for healthcare services on marginalized communities under Project 2025, it's essential to understand the far-reaching implications of such policy changes. Reduced funding in healthcare can significantly limit access to medical treatments for minority populations, exacerbating already prevalent health disparities. For instance, individuals from racial and ethnic minority communities often face systematic barriers that impede their ability to receive appropriate and timely healthcare.

Cuts in healthcare funding directly correlate with decreased access to necessary medical treatments, such as preventive care, specialist consultations, and emergency services. This lack of access can lead to a spike in untreated chronic diseases, which are disproportionately higher among minority populations. Conditions such as diabetes, hypertension, and heart disease are more prevalent in these communities, and without adequate funding, managing these conditions becomes increasingly difficult. Consequently, there is a potential for a deteriorating public health scenario where preventable conditions escalate into severe health crises.

Statistics highlight the gravity of this issue, showing markedly higher rates of health issues within minority communities. Studies have indicated that African Americans, Hispanic Americans, Native Americans, and other marginalized groups suffer from higher incidences of chronic illnesses. This trend suggests a long-term negative outcome if healthcare services continue to be underfunded. The direct correlation between healthcare accessibility and health outcomes underscores the need for robust healthcare funding as a preventative measure against worsening public health.

The urgency for equitable healthcare policies cannot be overstated. It is a moral imperative for government agencies to prioritize inclusive health reforms that consider the unique needs of marginalized communities. Equitable healthcare ensures that all populations receive fair treatment and access to healthcare services regardless of socioeconomic status or ethnic background. Government bodies must commit to creating and sustaining policies that bridge the gap in healthcare disparities, recognizing that the health of a community directly impacts its overall well-being and productivity.

Historical context offers valuable insights, demonstrating how past reforms successfully addressed healthcare disparities. For example, the Affordable Care Act (ACA), enacted in 2010, expanded Medicaid and established health insurance marketplaces, which provided millions of uninsured Americans with access to affordable healthcare. Research indicates that the ACA helped reduce disparities in health insurance coverage among racial and ethnic minorities, leading to improved health outcomes.

Another significant reform to consider is the establishment of community health centers, which have historically played a crucial role in delivering healthcare services to underserved populations. These centers provide comprehensive, high-quality care while addressing the social determinants of health that contribute to disparities. By investing in such models, we can draw parallels and identify strategic actions that can be implemented under Project 2025 to mitigate negative impacts.

Highlighting the detrimental effects of reduced healthcare funding is critical for mobilizing support for equitable policies. One approach is to engage in advocacy efforts that amplify the voices of those most affected by these cuts. Grassroots organizations, community leaders, and healthcare professionals must collaborate to raise awareness about the importance of sustained healthcare funding. Through concerted efforts, it is possible to influence policy decisions and ensure that marginalized communities are not left behind.

In addition to advocacy, investing in preventive care programs is essential. Preventive care reduces the incidence of chronic diseases by providing early interventions and promoting healthy lifestyles. Programs that focus on routine screenings, vaccinations, and health education can significantly improve health outcomes. Moreover, culturally competent care tailored to the specific needs of diverse communities can enhance patient engagement and ensure that healthcare services are accessible and effective.

Implementing telemedicine initiatives presents another viable solution. Telemedicine expands access to healthcare services, particularly for individuals in remote or underserved areas. During the COVID-19 pandemic, telemedicine emerged as a vital tool for maintaining continuity of care while minimizing exposure risks. By leveraging technology, healthcare providers can reach marginalized populations who may otherwise face barriers to accessing in-person care.

Furthermore, addressing systemic factors contributing to health disparities requires a multifaceted approach. Policymakers must consider the social determinants of health, including income inequality, education, housing, and environmental factors. Policies that address these underlying issues can create a more supportive environment for marginalized communities, ultimately improving their health outcomes.

A comparative analysis of successful past reforms also underscores the importance of data-driven approaches. Collecting and analyzing health data specific to minority populations can provide valuable insights into the unique challenges they face. This information can guide the development of targeted interventions and policies that address the root causes of health disparities.

To illustrate the potential impact of reduced healthcare funding, we can examine the COVID-19 pandemic response in different countries. Nations that invested in public health infrastructure and preparedness before the pandemic were better equipped to manage the crisis effectively. In contrast, the United States faced significant challenges due to chronic underinvestment in public health, resulting in disproportionate impacts on people of color and low-income communities (Johns & Rosenthal, 2022). This example highlights the need for sustained investments in healthcare to ensure resilience in the face of future health threats.

Chapter 15: Media and Information Control

Managing the media landscape and controlling the dissemination of information are at the heart of Project 2025's objectives. The potential ramifications of these actions extend beyond mere administrative adjustments, raising grave concerns about the future of free press and public discourse. With this project, the dynamics of who owns the media and how information flows to the public face unprecedented changes. Such transformations threaten to concentrate power in a few hands, reducing diversity in reporting and promoting a homogenized set of narratives. When only select voices dominate the conversation, democratic values can be severely compromised.

This chapter delves into various strategies that Project 2025 plans to employ to control media and information. From altering media ownership regulations to proposing licensing for journalists, each approach has far-reaching implications for journalistic independence and public transparency. The discussion includes examples from other countries where similar measures have led to detrimental outcomes, providing a sobering look at what might lie ahead. Additionally, the chapter will examine the potential impacts of investigative journalism and the risks associated with promoting state-sponsored media voices. Overall, this exploration aims to shed light on the critical nature of maintaining a diverse and independent media landscape in safeguarding democracy.

Control and Regulation of Media Outlets

Media and Information Control

Project 2025 aims to regulate media outlets in ways that raise significant concerns about democratic communication and pluralism. The proposed changes in media ownership regulations are among the most critical of these initiatives. By altering how ownership is distributed, the project could lead to a concentration of media power in fewer hands. This would reduce the diversity of reporting sources and viewpoints, making the media landscape more homogeneous and less reflective of an array of perspectives. When a few entities control the majority of media outlets, they can influence public opinion, marginalizing dissenting voices and promoting narratives that align with their agendas.

For instance, imagine if only a handful of companies controlled all major news networks, newspapers, and digital platforms in the country. These organizations would have the power to decide which stories get attention and which ones do not, effectively shaping the public discourse to fit a particular point of view. It's not just about what gets reported but also how it gets reported. The tone, framing, and even omission of stories can significantly affect public perception. When media ownership is concentrated, the risk of these biases becoming entrenched increases dramatically.

This issue of concentrated media ownership is not theoretical. It has already happened in several countries, where monopolistic control over media has led to reduced journalistic independence and a lack of investigative reporting. In such environments, news often becomes a tool of propaganda rather than a means of informing the public (Media, 2023). The implications for democracy are dire, as a well-informed citizenry is crucial for meaningful participation in governance.

In addition to concentrating on media ownership, Project 2025 proposes licensing and certifying journalists. At first glance, this might seem like a move toward ensuring quality and professionalism in journalism. However, consider the consequences of placing the power to license journalists under government control. Such a system could easily be used to exclude independent and critical voices from the media landscape. Journalists who challenge the government's narrative or expose corruption could find themselves without a license, effectively silencing them.

Unchecked oversight of journalism can undermine accountability by turning media into an arm of the state rather than a watchdog for the public. Imagine a scenario where only government-approved journalists are allowed to report on significant events. The potential for bias and manipulation becomes apparent. This kind of control can stifle investigative journalism, which is essential for uncovering truths that those in power might prefer to keep hidden.

Consider the case of countries where journalist licensing is already in place. In these nations, press freedom is often severely restricted, and journalists operate under the constant threat of losing their ability to report if they cross certain lines. This environment leads to self-censorship, where journalists avoid covering controversial topics for fear of reprisal. The long-term effect is a less informed public and a weakened democracy, as citizens lose access to diverse perspectives and critical information (United States Department of State, 2022).

Another alarming strategy proposed by Project 2025 is the promotion of state-sponsored media voices. While having some government-backed media outlets is not inherently problematic, the danger lies in allowing these voices to dominate the media space. State-sponsored media can quickly become echo chambers that drown out independent perspectives, creating an imbalanced public discourse. In a healthy democracy, the media should serve as a forum for a variety of viewpoints. When state-sponsored voices overshadow others, the result is a one-dimensional narrative that does not reflect the complexity of real-world issues.

Echo chambers are particularly dangerous because they reinforce existing beliefs and discourage critical thinking. When people are only exposed to information that confirms their existing views, they become less open to alternative perspectives. This phenomenon is already evident on social media platforms, where algorithms tend to show users content similar to what they've interacted with before, creating a bubble of homogeneity. If state-sponsored media were to follow this trend, the public would become increasingly insulated from diverse viewpoints, further polarizing society.

Moreover, state-sponsored media can serve as a tool for spreading propaganda. With the government's backing, these outlets can push narratives that support authoritarian goals, undermining democratic values and institutions. For instance, they might downplay government failures or amplify achievements, skewing public perception. In extreme cases, they can be used to vilify opposition groups, activists, and even ordinary citizens who dissent. This creates a culture of fear and conformity, where challenging the status quo becomes increasingly dangerous.

The dangers posed by these strategies need to be understood within the broader context of democratic communication and pluralism. A free and independent press is one of the cornerstones of any democratic society. It provides a platform for debate, holds power accountable, and ensures that citizens are well-informed about matters of public interest. When media control is centralized, and journalistic freedom is curtailed, these functions are compromised. The result is a less vibrant democracy, where public discourse is impoverished, and political participation is diminished.

Potential for Surveillance of Media Content

The monitoring of media outputs, as proposed under Project 2025, carries profound implications for the free press and public discourse. Increased surveillance of journalists is one significant concern. When journalists know they are being closely monitored, they may limit their reporting to avoid potential repercussions. This self-censorship undermines the very essence of journalism, which is to inform the public without fear or favor.

Surveillance often creates an atmosphere of intimidation. Journalists might refrain from covering controversial topics or critical news that could be seen as opposing government views. The result is a less informed public, shielded from information crucial to democratic decision-making processes. As highlighted by Irene Khan, the UN Special Rapporteur for freedom of expression, this erosion of media freedom strikes at the heart of democracy (Huang, 2024). Fear of reprisal can lead to a homogeneous media landscape where challenging the status quo becomes increasingly rare.

Additionally, the mass-flagging or removal of content poses another threat to journalistic integrity. Algorithms designed to flag or remove supposedly harmful content can often misinterpret context, leading to the unwarranted suppression of valid journalistic work. Such actions disrupt the flow of truthful information and create gaps in the narrative that are detrimental to public understanding. This mechanized approach to content regulation fails to appreciate the nuances inherent in journalistic reporting.

The statistical data presented by Reporters Without Borders in their 2023 World Press Freedom Index indicates that more than half of the countries assessed are unsafe for journalists, with many operating under difficult or very serious conditions (Huang, 2024). In regions where media is heavily controlled, automated systems for content removal can become tools for authoritarian governance to quash dissent and control public perception.

Furthermore, policies targeting dissenting opinions contribute significantly to public disillusionment with the media. When governments employ strategies to mute contrary perspectives, the credibility of the media suffers. Consistent efforts to stifle opposition not only diminish trust but also provoke skepticism about the fairness and independence of journalists. This erosion of trust paves the way for misinformation and propaganda to flourish, complicating efforts to foster an informed citizenry.

For instance, Maria Ressa's experiences in the Philippines illustrate the dangers posed by weaponized laws against the free press. Her arrest on multiple charges, perceived as politically motivated actions against her criticism of the government, exemplifies how dissenting voices can be targeted through legal avenues (Huang, 2024). Such policies send a chilling message to other journalists, potential whistleblowers, and activists who may choose silence over persecution.

This pattern of suppressing dissent is resonant worldwide, particularly in regions where democracy is backsliding. The normalization of censorship, whether through overt governmental policies or subtler means like social pressure and economic sanctions, underscores a growing threat to free expression. Authoritarian regimes benefit from a muzzled press, manipulating public narratives to maintain power and control. Civil societies play a crucial role in counteracting these tendencies by raising awareness and holding leaders accountable. Organizations like Forbidden Stories ensure that even silenced journalists have their stories told, maintaining a semblance of transparency and promoting global accountability (Huang, 2024).

Moreover, surveillance has far-reaching implications beyond direct intimidation of journalists. It affects the broader public's willingness to engage in open discourse. When individuals believe their every word or action online is monitored, they self-censor to avoid becoming targets of scrutiny. This phenomenon was evident in the U.S. when international filmmakers chose to curb their political statements on social media, fearing visa denial or retaliatory measures (Levinson-Waldman et al., 2022). This chilling effect stifles not just political speech but also creative and cultural expressions crucial for a vibrant society.

Policies enforcing mass surveillance and content regulation must be scrutinized for their impact on free expression. The Brennan Center's lawsuit against the State Department and DHS illustrates how such measures can lead to widespread self-censorship (Levinson-Waldman et al., 2022). When journalists and ordinary citizens alike curtail their speech due to fear of governmental retaliation, the quality and breadth of public debate suffer immensely.

Thus, while the motives behind increased monitoring of media outputs may be framed as protecting public order or national security, the consequences extend much further. The integrity of journalism, the plurality of voices in the media, and the robustness of public discourse are all at stake. The transition towards normalizing censorship threatens core democratic values, requiring vigilant resistance and robust legal frameworks to protect free expression.

Combating "Fake News" and Misinformation

The framing of 'fake news' has emerged as a significant tool for authoritarian regimes to control the media landscape and manage the dissemination of information. This tactic can be particularly effective in undermining democratic discourse, as it allows those in power to discredit legitimate reporting that challenges or contradicts government narratives. Labeling dissenting voices as purveyors of 'fake news' provides a convenient way to dismiss critical perspectives without having to engage with their substance.

In many cases, the term 'fake news' is weaponized to create a hostile environment against independent journalism. When government officials or state-sponsored media repeatedly accuse credible journalists and media outlets of spreading falsehoods, it fosters public skepticism toward these sources. Consequently, this undermines the role of the press in holding authorities accountable and diminishes the quality of public discourse. For example, in various countries around the world, laws purportedly designed to combat 'fake news' have led to the arrest and prosecution of journalists and citizens for their online and offline expressions. Such actions deter investigative reporting and discourage individuals from expressing dissenting opinions.

Government-led fact-checking initiatives are another dimension where biases can emerge. While these programs are often presented as efforts to safeguard the truth, they are susceptible to manipulation by those in power. By claiming the authority to arbitrarily determine what constitutes 'true' and 'false' information, governments can easily skew perceptions to align with their interests. Fact-checking bodies that lack independence may unfairly target opposition figures or controversial topics that are politically sensitive. This creates an environment where the filter through which information passes becomes tainted by partisan influences, rather than objective scrutiny.

Moreover, there is always a risk of misjudgment in fact-checking, leading to the dissemination of inaccurate assertions that can mislead the public. Even well-intentioned fact-checkers can make errors, especially in rapidly evolving situations where information is fluid. These mistakes can distract from vital issues by focusing attention on debunking or confirming specific claims rather than addressing the underlying problems. For instance, during public health crises or political scandals, the emphasis may shift to the veracity of individual statements rather than the broader implications or policy responses needed.

Censorship of information labeled as misinformation presents another significant threat to democratic discourse. Governments often wield the accusation of 'spreading misinformation' as a pretext to suppress opposing viewpoints. By doing so, they curtail the diversity of perspectives necessary for an informed public debate. In societies where censorship prevails, the public receives a homogenized version of reality that mirrors the government's stance, leaving little room for alternative narratives. This controlled flow of information stifles critical thinking and inhibits the societal progress that stems from robust debate.

Censorship also carries the risk of creating echo chambers where only conforming voices are amplified, and dissenting ones are silenced. This phenomenon polarizes communities, as individuals are less likely to encounter viewpoints that challenge their beliefs. Echo chambers reinforce existing biases and contribute to the spread of propaganda, making it easier for authoritarian regimes to maintain control over the populace. When people are not exposed to diverse opinions, they become more susceptible to believing state-driven narratives without question. For instance, in countries like China and Russia, state-controlled media overwhelmingly dominate the information ecosystem, shaping public perception in ways that favor the government.

Indeed, the manufactured fear of misinformation can condition populations to accept increased regulation and surveillance without protest. Under the guise of protecting the public from harmful falsehoods, governments can implement policies that grant them sweeping powers to monitor and control internet activity. These measures often come at the expense of individual privacy and freedom of expression. The surveillance capitalism model, where major technology platforms monetize user data, further exacerbates this issue by enabling precise microtargeting of messages. Authoritarian regimes can exploit these capabilities to shape public opinion and suppress dissent efficiently.

Furthermore, authoritarian regimes are quick to adapt techniques from one another, refining their strategies to better control information both domestically and internationally. The global landscape has seen a rise in sophisticated state actors, such as China and Russia, employing computational propaganda for foreign influence operations. This practice involves the use of algorithms and social media manipulation to disseminate disinformation, incite polarization, and undermine trust in democratic institutions. Studies by organizations like the Oxford Internet Institute have highlighted how these regimes collaborate and share best practices to amplify their impact.

It is also crucial to consider the psychological drivers behind the consumption of disinformation. Deeply polarized societies with low trust in media are particularly vulnerable to the appeal of emotionally or ideologically validating content. People tend to seek out information that confirms their preexisting beliefs, making them more likely to share and perpetuate misleading content. This dynamic serves the interests of authoritarian regimes, as it aids in strengthening their narrative while weakening democratic resilience.

The consequences of these trends are far-reaching. As the credibility of independent media erodes and public trust diminishes, the foundations of democracy itself come under threat. A well-informed citizenry is essential for meaningful participation in democratic processes. When access to accurate information is compromised, individuals are deprived of the knowledge required to make informed decisions. This erosion of democratic discourse ultimately benefits authoritarian regimes, which thrive in environments where dissent is minimized, and public perception is tightly controlled.

Rallying Public Support Against Misinformation

Efforts to combat misinformation have emerged as a significant tool for rallying public support under the guise of consumer security. Governments claim that these measures are necessary to protect citizens from harmful content, yet in many cases, they serve authoritarian motives. Under the banner of fighting fake news, states may promote policies that ultimately erode individual freedoms and democratic norms. For example, according to *The Rise of Digital Authoritarianism: Fake News, Data Collection and the Challenge to Democracy* (2018), various governments worldwide have enacted or proposed laws restricting online media, citing the need to curb disinformation. These laws give authorities wide discretion to determine what constitutes "misinformation," potentially silencing dissenting voices and independent journalism.

Manipulating public perception is another strategy often employed to divert attention from harmful practices and policies. When governments frame their actions as protective measures against misinformation, they can obscure the true intent behind legislation and regulation that infringe on personal liberties. Misinformation laws, touted as tools for national security, can become instruments for consolidating power and stifling political opposition. This manipulation not only misleads the public but also creates a false sense of unity and consensus, masking the authoritarian underpinnings of such policies. In Russia, for instance, the government used fake news laws to arrest journalists and human rights activists, thereby controlling the narrative around the conflict in Ukraine (Reuters Citation2022).

Encouraging fear of misinformation can condition populations to accept increased regulation and surveillance without protest. By highlighting the dangers of fake news, authorities can generate a climate of fear that justifies intrusive measures. Governments argue that stringent oversight is essential for preventing the spread of false information that could cause social unrest or harm public health. However, this heightened state of vigilance often leads to more invasive surveillance and data collection practices, which are rarely subject to adequate scrutiny or oversight. As noted in *The Rise of Digital Authoritarianism: Fake News, Data Collection and the Challenge to Democracy* (2018), several countries have intensified state surveillance, weakening encryption and accessing personal data without proper safeguards. Such actions compromise civil liberties and privacy while conditioning citizens to view surveillance as a necessary evil.

State efforts to promote specific narratives also play a crucial role in undermining trust in authentic news sources. When the government controls the flow of information, it can flood the media landscape with state-sponsored narratives, rendering independent journalism less credible and harder to access. Propaganda and disinformation campaigns further muddy the waters, making it increasingly difficult for the public to discern truth from falsehood. In 32 out of 65 countries studied, government actors manipulated online discussions to favor government perspectives (*The Rise of Digital Authoritarianism: Fake News, Data Collection and the Challenge to Democracy*, 2018). This manipulation not only skews public opinion but also erodes faith in the media, contributing to a decline in internet freedom and democratic discourse.

The use of legal frameworks to combat misinformation can be particularly insidious. By enacting laws that criminalize the dissemination of false information, governments gain powerful tools to repress dissent. These laws often carry severe penalties, deterring journalists and activists from exposing governmental malfeasance. The chilling effect on free speech is pronounced, as individuals and media outlets self-censor to avoid potential repercussions. In nations like Singapore and Indonesia, fake news laws are justified on the grounds of maintaining social harmony and national security (Ong & Chew Citation2019). However, these laws grant the state sweeping powers to revoke media licenses and censor content, fundamentally altering the media landscape and diminishing democratic engagement.

Moreover, the weaponization of terms like "fake news" serves to delegitimize genuine journalism and critique. Political leaders and governments adopt this rhetoric to dismiss or discredit reporting that contradicts official statements, muddying the waters of public discourse. Former U.S. President Donald Trump popularized the use of "fake news" to denigrate unfavorable coverage, a tactic now mirrored by politicians globally (Wardle & Derakhshan Citation2017). This strategy undermines journalistic norms and fosters a climate where the credibility of news organizations is continually challenged, further complicating the task of holding power to account.

In addition to legal and rhetorical strategies, governments employ sophisticated digital tactics to control narratives. Pro-government bots and trolls are deployed to manipulate online conversations, spreading favorable propaganda while drowning out opposing viewpoints. Social media platforms, once heralded as democratizing forces, become battlegrounds for information control. According to *The Rise of Digital Authoritarianism: Fake News, Data Collection and the Challenge to Democracy* (2018), these practices have shifted from open platforms like Facebook to more closed messaging apps, making them harder to detect and counteract. The resultant cacophony of voices makes it challenging for accurate and reliable information to emerge, further entrenching state control over public perception.

Efforts to combat misinformation often masquerade as well-intentioned initiatives but carry significant risks for democratic societies. While the stated goal may be to protect citizens from harmful content, the reality is frequently an expansion of state power at the expense of individual freedoms. Manipulating public perception, fostering fear, and promoting state-approved narratives weaken the foundational principles of free press and open discourse. As governments continue to refine these tactics, politically active individuals, academics, environmentalists, and social justice advocates must remain vigilant. Understanding these dynamics is crucial for developing effective strategies for resistance and preserving the integrity of democratic institutions.

Insights and Implications

Project 2025's strategies for media control pose a significant threat to democratic values and the free press. By concentrating media ownership, licensing journalists, promoting state-sponsored media, and increasing surveillance, the project risks creating a media landscape that is less diverse and more biased. Such measures can undermine journalistic independence and reduce the availability of diverse viewpoints, vital for a well-informed public. In an environment where dissenting voices are marginalized, public discourse suffers, making it easier for those in power to push their narratives without accountability.

These proposed changes to media oversight and content regulation highlight the broader danger of eroding democratic principles under the guise of maintaining order and combating misinformation. Centralizing media control, labeling unfavorable reports as 'fake news,' and leveraging surveillance tactics not only stifle free speech but also foster self-censorship among journalists and citizens alike. This environment breeds conformity and reduces critical engagement, ultimately weakening the pillars of democracy. It is imperative to remain vigilant and advocate for a media landscape that supports diversity and independent journalism, ensuring robust democratic participation and accountability.

Chapter 16: Judicial Implications

Understanding the judicial implications of Project 2025 involves examining how potential changes in the judiciary could impact democratic principles and civil liberties. In particular, this chapter delves into the ways strategic appointments of conservative judges might reshape legal interpretations, influencing pivotal areas such as reproductive rights, voting laws, and free speech. These shifts can affect not only the highest courts but also trickle down to federal and state levels, thereby altering the entire judicial landscape for generations.

This chapter will discuss various facets of these judicial changes, including the ideological leanings of appointed judges and their broader societal impacts. It will explore how these appointments may lead to a judiciary that prioritizes corporate interests over individual rights and examine the potential consequences for marginalized communities. Additionally, the chapter will analyze the threats posed by reduced judicial diversity and the erosion of checks and balances within the system. Through a critical narrative, readers will gain insight into the expansive reach of judicial decisions and the necessity for vigilant advocacy to uphold democratic values and civil liberties.

Appointment of Conservative Judges

Strategic appointments of conservative judges can profoundly reshape legal interpretations and impact civil rights. This assertion is underscored by the role these judges play in ruling on pivotal cases affecting key rights such as reproductive health, voting, and free speech.

Conservative judges tend to interpret the Constitution through an originalist or textualist lens, meaning they focus on the intent of the framers and the literal text rather than evolving social norms. This approach often leads to decisions that restrict reproductive rights, limit access to abortion services, and uphold stringent voter identification laws. In addition, rulings on free speech may prioritize traditional values over modern expressions of dissent and protest, affecting minority voices disproportionately.

The selection process for these judges can be highly politicized, emphasizing ideological conformity over judicial independence. When appointments are made based on a candidate's alignment with prevailing conservative ideologies, the judiciary may become less protective of civil liberties. For instance, judges who adhere strictly to conservative views may be less inclined to support rulings that protect LGBTQ+ rights or defend affirmative action policies. These decisions can erode protections that have been established over decades, potentially leading to a significant rollback of civil liberties (Bazelon, 2024).

Moreover, the influence of corporate interests in judicial appointments raises concerns about the balance of justice. Conservative judges often favor corporations in their rulings, siding with business interests over individual rights. Such decisions can affect regulations protecting consumers, the environment, and workers' rights. A judiciary that consistently rules in favor of corporate entities risks distorting justice and undermining public trust in the legal system (Conservatives and the Court, n.d.).

Additionally, the potential for unanimous conservative judicial decisions poses a threat to marginalized communities. When the majority of judges share similar ideological perspectives, their decisions can solidify precedents that disadvantage vulnerable groups. Historical examples demonstrate how courts can use precedent-setting decisions to maintain systemic inequalities. For example, rulings that support restrictive immigration policies or limit access to welfare can disproportionately impact immigrant populations and low-income families. The consolidation of conservative viewpoints in the judiciary thus has long-term implications for social equity and justice.

A critical examination of recent judicial trends reveals the tangible effects of such appointments. The "history and tradition" test, recently adopted by the Supreme Court's conservative majority, serves as a tool for setting aside modern developments in the law in favor of historical precedents. This trend is evident in rulings that challenge progressive movements like the expansion of LGBTQ+ rights, gun control measures, and reproductive freedoms. By invoking history and tradition, conservative judges can effectively turn back the clock on social advancements, impacting the daily lives of millions of Americans (Bazelon, 2024).

Furthermore, the erosion of judicial independence can lead to an increased perception of partisanship within the judiciary. As judges are seen more as political actors than impartial arbiters of the law, public confidence in the judicial system may diminish. This dynamic creates an environment where court decisions are viewed through a partisan lens, fueling polarization and undermining the legitimacy of the judiciary. Historically, the American legal system has thrived on its commitment to fairness and objectivity; however, the current trajectory threatens to destabilize this foundation.

Conservative judicial appointments also carry significant implications for environmental regulations and climate policy. Judges who prioritize economic over ecological considerations may rule against regulations aimed at curbing pollution or mitigating climate change. For instance, decisions that favor the deregulation of industries can lead to increased environmental degradation and hinder efforts to combat global warming. The ramifications of such rulings extend beyond national borders, contributing to global environmental challenges and exacerbating social injustices faced by communities vulnerable to climate impacts.

Civil liberties, particularly those related to personal freedoms, face significant jeopardy under a predominantly conservative judiciary. Issues like privacy rights, digital freedoms, and surveillance policies could see regressive changes. Conservative judges might endorse broader governmental surveillance powers at the expense of individual privacy rights, justifying such decisions on grounds of national security. This shift could pave the way for invasive policies that encroach on personal freedoms and normalize state intrusion into private lives.

Moreover, the jurisprudence shaped by conservative judges often reflects a resistance to progressive interpretations of equality and justice. For example, debates over affirmative action policies illustrate how conservative rulings can curtail efforts to address historical discrimination. Judicial decisions that overturn or weaken affirmative action policies impact educational and professional opportunities for marginalized groups, perpetuating cycles of inequality.

Unquestionably, the strategic appointment of conservative judges reshapes the legal landscape in ways that reach far beyond specific cases. It molds the judiciary into an instrument that can systematically favor particular ideologies, thereby influencing the direction of societal progress. The consolidation of conservative power within the judiciary presents a critical juncture for advocates of democratic principles and civil rights. Understanding these dynamics is essential for those invested in preserving and advancing civil liberties and justice in the face of evolving judicial philosophies.

Recognizing the transformative influence of judicial appointments underscores the necessity for vigilant advocacy and informed citizen engagement. Progressive and liberal stakeholders must challenge efforts to undermine judicial independence and ensure that the judiciary remains a bastion of objective and fair decision-making. This endeavor necessitates a robust commitment to monitoring judicial appointments, advocating for transparency in the selection process, and fostering public awareness about the implications of judicial rulings on civil rights and liberties.

Long-Term Effects on Lower Courts

The cascading effects of Supreme Court appointments on federal and state courts can be profound, reshaping the judiciary's landscape for generations. When a president makes successive appointments to the Supreme Court, it’s not just the highest court in the land that feels the impact; the ideological tilt can establish an ethos that permeates throughout the entire judicial system.

One significant consequence is the potential erasure of decades of progressive rulings. When conservative justices dominate the Supreme Court, their decisions often ripple down to lower courts, influencing interpretations of the law in ways that align with conservative ideals. This trend can reverse progressive legal advancements in areas such as civil rights, environmental protections, and workers' rights. The 2005 Supreme Court decision in United States v. Booker, which increased judges' discretion in sentencing, showcases how shifts in the Supreme Court’s composition can alter long-standing legal practices. This decision widened sentencing disparities, reflecting the influence of judicial ideology on everyday rulings (Bias on the Bench, 2019).

Judicial vacancies filled by ideological allies further entrench these changes across the country. Politically motivated selections can lead to anti-democratic rulings that conflict with the broader public interest. For example, efforts by Senate Majority Leader Mitch McConnell to prioritize conservative judicial appointments have created a judiciary more likely to issue rulings that favor restrictive voting laws or limit reproductive rights (Root & Berger, 2019). These appointments don't just affect landmark cases but also shape the outcomes of countless lesser-known cases, cumulatively altering the judicial landscape.

A crucial issue arises when partisan affiliation supersedes judicial qualifications in the appointment process, risking the erosion of public faith in the legal system. Judges are expected to be impartial arbiters of justice, but when they are chosen primarily for their political leanings, it undermines confidence in their ability to administer fair and unbiased judgments. According to research by Alma Cohen and Crystal Yang, there is substantial evidence that judicial politics play a considerable role in perpetuating racial and gender disparities in sentencing (Bias on the Bench, 2019). Such findings highlight how partisan appointments can exacerbate existing inequalities within the legal system.

A politicized judiciary is another concerning factor. When judges make decisions based on partisan bias rather than constitutional interpretation, it distorts the justice system. Decisions may reflect the ideologies of the appointing power rather than the merits of the case. This results in a judiciary that could be less protective of civil liberties, more permissive of governmental overreach, and inclined to favor corporate interests over individual rights. Justice Neil Gorsuch famously declared there's no such thing as Republican or Democratic judges, yet the reality often contradicts this ideal (Bias on the Bench, 2019). Research consistently shows that judges appointed by different parties tend to rule differently on similar cases, indicating persistent partisan influences.

To illustrate these points, examine the shift during recent administrations. During President Trump's tenure, his administration focused heavily on filling federal court vacancies with conservative judges. This strategy has had long-term implications, including the establishment of precedents that may prove difficult to overturn. These judges are more likely to rule in ways that align with conservative views, impacting decisions on issues ranging from campaign finance to environmental regulations (Root & Berger, 2019). The composition of the courts thus becomes a determining factor in the direction of U.S. policy and law.

Moreover, the appointment process itself has become increasingly polarized. The elimination of traditional processes like blue slips, which allowed senators to block nominations from their states, exemplifies how partisan tactics can erode longstanding norms. By sidelining input from the American Bar Association and other nonpartisan entities, the focus has shifted entirely to ideological alignment (Bias on the Bench, 2019). This approach heightens the risk of appointing judges who lack the requisite experience or demonstrate overt biases, diminishing the quality and impartiality of the judiciary.

This politicization extends beyond the federal level, affecting state courts as well. State judiciaries often look to federal courts for guidance, particularly on constitutional matters. When the Supreme Court sets a precedent, state courts frequently follow suit. Consequently, a federal judiciary skewed towards conservatism can prompt similar trends at the state level, leading to uniformly conservative interpretations of laws across various jurisdictions. This uniformity can stifle legal diversity and reduce the availability of alternative legal perspectives.

Additionally, the emphasis on partisan loyalty over judicial expertise threatens to undermine the foundational principle of an independent judiciary. A judiciary perceived as politically biased loses its moral authority and legitimacy in the eyes of the public. This loss of trust can discourage citizens from seeking legal recourse and complying with judicial decisions, thereby weakening the rule of law.

Furthermore, structural issues within the judicial system exacerbate these problems. Conservative lawmakers have been highly effective in shaping the courts, and implementing procedural rules that limit access to justice for vulnerable groups. By restricting plaintiffs' abilities to bring class action lawsuits and expanding forced arbitration, they have effectively minimized the courts' role as a venue for holding powerful entities accountable. These changes disproportionately affect low-income individuals and marginalized communities, entrenching systemic inequalities (Root & Berger, 2019).

Changes to Federal Court Jurisdictions

Proposed alterations to federal court jurisdictions under Project 2025 stand to erode the inherent checks and balances that safeguard democratic principles. The strategic manipulation of court jurisdictions may lead to fewer checks on executive power, thereby enabling greater governmental overreach. This alteration means that executive actions could bypass thorough judicial review, allowing potentially unconstitutional policies to go unchecked. For example, if certain types of cases are reassigned to courts with known biases, it becomes easier for the executive branch to implement controversial measures without the fear of judicial pushback.

A crucial aspect of sustaining an impartial judiciary is maintaining diverse viewpoints among judges. However, a streamlined process for conservative agendas threatens this diversity. When federal courts lean heavily toward one ideological perspective, decisions tend to reflect less on public interest and more on the maintenance of particular political ideologies. This lack of judicial diversity can lead to rulings that predominantly support conservative policies, diminishing the broad representation of the populace's varied interests. A judiciary lacking in ideological balance may neglect the needs of different communities, leading to skewed interpretations of law that do not serve the general public fairly.

Moreover, narrowing the jurisdiction of federal courts restricts avenues available for individuals wanting to challenge civil rights violations. Fewer courts with the authority to hear such cases mean limited opportunities for redress, making it more cumbersome for citizens to fight against infringement upon their rights. This is particularly concerning for marginalized groups that rely on the ability to bring lawsuits as a means of challenging systemic injustices. Restricted court access exacerbates existing inequalities by shielding discriminatory practices from judicial scrutiny. Consequently, efforts to combat racial, economic, and gender discrimination face significant hurdles, further entrenching social inequities.

Marginalized individuals often already struggle with limited resources to pursue justice. Proposed changes reducing pathways to the courts can escalate this problem, leading to systemic disenfranchisement. Many people may find themselves unable to afford prolonged legal battles, especially when faced with a narrower selection of courts willing or able to hear their cases. The expense and complexity associated with navigating fewer, possibly more distant, courts deter those without financial means from seeking legal recourse. This development risks creating a two-tiered justice system where only the affluent have the means to fight for their rights effectively.

Federal courts have traditionally served as crucial venues for resolving disputes involving the government and protecting individual rights (United States Courts, 2019). Changes that limit these functions fundamentally alter the relationship between the judiciary and the citizenry. By reducing the accountability of courts to the broader population, there is a danger of fostering an environment where governmental actions remain unchecked and unchallenged. Executive overreach can become institutionalized, with long-term implications for democratic norms and governance.

To illustrate the tangible impact of such jurisdictional changes, consider how narrowing the scope of federal courts affects bankruptcy law. Federal courts have exclusive jurisdiction over all bankruptcy cases as determined by Congress (United States Courts, 2019). Imagine a scenario where similar exclusivity applies broadly to various civil rights issues, but only conservative-leaning courts possess this authority. It would make it significantly harder for progressive interpretations of the law to gain traction, inevitably biasing the outcomes toward specific political doctrines.

One prominent concern is the diminished judicial diversity, which can influence societal values. A judiciary dominated by a single ideological faction fails to represent the heterogeneous nature of society. Supreme Court Justice Ruth Bader Ginsburg once highlighted the importance of a diverse bench in ensuring that different life experiences inform judicial decisions. Eroding this diversity not only undermines public trust but also erodes the quality of justice dispensed. Decisions rooted in a narrow ideological spectrum fail to capture the complexities of modern society, resulting in overly simplistic and potentially harmful legal precedents.

The systematic disenfranchisement of marginalized communities through restricted access to justice underscores a monumental issue. When courts lose their capacity to serve as arbiters for all, they fail their fundamental purpose. Those most in need of protection—the economically disadvantaged, racial minorities, and other vulnerable groups—suffer the most. Without adequate avenues to contest injustices, these groups face prolonged oppression and inequality.

In addition to limiting courtroom access, reduced jurisdictions affect the broader ecosystem of legal advocacy. Public interest law firms and non-profit organizations that depend on robust federal courts to challenge unjust laws will encounter substantial barriers. These entities provide essential services in fighting for civil liberties and environmental protection. Curtailing their ability to file suits at the federal level weakens the overall infrastructure designed to uphold democratic values and protect civil rights.

As we analyze the overarching consequences of altering federal court jurisdictions, it becomes evident that any reduction compromises the judiciary's role in maintaining balance within the government structure. The integrity of the judicial process relies on its independence and its capacity to offer an unbiased review of executive and legislative actions. Project 2025's proposed changes risk transforming courts into mere instruments of political will, stripping them of their essential role as a check on power.

Resistance and Accountability

Exploration of potential mobilization efforts to counteract these judicial shifts is crucial in maintaining democratic principles and civil liberties. As judicial changes loom under Project 2025, it's imperative to consider grassroots initiatives that may emerge in response to perceived injustices. These community-driven movements can serve as a powerful force in holding judges accountable and ensuring that the judiciary remains fair and impartial.

Grassroots initiatives often begin at the local level, where citizens are most directly affected by judicial decisions. Community organizations can mobilize to monitor court proceedings, advocate for ethical behavior from judges, and create platforms for public awareness about judicial misconduct. By doing so, they can help maintain a check on the judiciary and deter any attempts to undermine democratic values. For instance, local watchdog groups can organize campaigns to raise awareness about particular judges' track records, encouraging the public to take a more active role in judicial oversight.

Public advocacy for transparency in the appointment process is another effective mobilization effort. Transparency ensures that the selection of judges is free from undue influence and reflects the diversity and values of the broader society. Advocates can push for clear criteria and processes for judicial nominations, making it harder for partisan agendas to dominate. This includes demanding open hearings, publishing nominee backgrounds, and requiring comprehensive disclosure of potential conflicts of interest. Such measures create pressure on appointing bodies to consider a wider pool of candidates, thus promoting a more balanced judiciary.

Educating citizens about the implications of judicial appointments is essential for fostering an engaged electorate. When people understand how judicial decisions can impact their daily lives and broader societal norms, they are more likely to participate in the electoral process and hold appointed officials accountable. Educational campaigns can include workshops, seminars, and online resources that explain the judiciary's role and the long-term effects of judicial appointments. By equipping citizens with knowledge, these initiatives empower them to challenge rulings that threaten democratic principles and civil liberties.

The importance of public education cannot be overstated. Informed citizens can critically evaluate judicial actions and mobilize against decisions that may curtail rights and freedoms. Historical instances provide valuable lessons in this regard. History is replete with examples where significant legal battles were fought to preserve judicial independence and integrity. Examining these cases can offer insights into current challenges and strategies for resistance. For example, the landmark case of Brown v. Board of Education reveals the judiciary's potential to enact profound social change, but also the persistent need for vigilance to protect such gains.

Grassroots initiatives and public advocacy aren't just theoretical concepts; they have practical, real-world applications. Take, for instance, the rise of grassroots organizations like the American Civil Liberties Union (ACLU), which consistently fights against judicial overreach and works to protect individual rights. These organizations provide a model for new movements seeking to counteract judicial shifts. They demonstrate how coordinated efforts, strategic litigation, and public outreach can successfully challenge policies that undermine democratic norms.

Mobilizing efforts should also include leveraging modern technology to enhance civic participation. Social media platforms can amplify calls for judicial accountability and transparency, allowing advocates to reach broader audiences quickly. Online petitions, virtual town halls, and digital campaigns can gather support and put pressure on decision-makers to uphold ethical standards in judiciary appointments. Additionally, providing digital tools and resources can help citizens engage more effectively with the judicial system, ensuring their voices are heard.

Transparency in judicial appointments doesn't just stop at the selection process; it extends to ongoing accountability measures. Regular audits of judicial performance and the publication of these findings can maintain high standards within the judiciary. Publicly available data on judges' rulings, reversal rates, and adherence to ethical guidelines can inform citizens and policymakers alike, contributing to a more informed and vigilant public. This level of scrutiny helps to discourage unethical behavior and promotes judicial fairness.

It's also important to consider the role of independent commissions in recommending judicial nominees. By removing some of the selection process from direct political control, these bodies can ensure that nominees are evaluated based on merit rather than allegiance to a particular ideology. Independent commissions can assess candidates' qualifications, past rulings, and potential biases, providing a safeguard against partisan manipulation. This approach can help restore public trust in the judiciary by emphasizing competence and integrity over political loyalty.

The history of judicial challenges shows that resilience in the face of adversity is possible. The judiciary has often been a battleground for larger political and social struggles. Reflecting on historical cases where jurisdictional changes faced significant legal battles can inspire contemporary efforts to defend judicial independence. For instance, the New Deal-era battles between President Franklin D. Roosevelt and the Supreme Court illustrate how determined advocacy and strategic reforms can shape the judiciary and its role in democracy.

Chapter 17: Mobilizing Against Project 2025

Mobilizing against Project 2025 requires strategic planning and grassroots efforts to resist its proposed policies. This chapter delves into the crucial tactics that activists and concerned citizens can employ to counteract these agendas effectively. From organizing community engagement workshops to leveraging social media, the chapter lays out a comprehensive framework for building strong networks of resistance. It emphasizes the importance of local action networks and coalition-building across diverse communities, highlighting how these methods are integral to fostering democratic values and promoting widespread opposition.

In this chapter, readers will explore various grassroots organizing techniques designed to educate and mobilize individuals. The chapter outlines the steps necessary for creating impactful community workshops that equip participants with essential advocacy skills. It also covers the development of local action networks that facilitate information exchange and collaborative efforts among activists. The effective use of social media as a tool for advocacy is discussed, providing insights into how digital platforms can amplify the resistance movement. Additionally, the chapter highlights the power of petitions and public statements in exerting pressure on decision-makers. Through these strategies, the chapter aims to empower activists with the knowledge and tools needed for sustained resistance against Project 2025.

Grassroots Organizing Tactics

Community Engagement Workshops serve as a cornerstone for grassroots organizing. These workshops focus on educating community members about Project 2025 and its potential impacts, allowing them to voice their concerns, and more crucially, training participants in essential advocacy skills. The primary aim is to ensure that individuals are well-equipped to engage in political discourse effectively. Workshops can cover various topics such as understanding legislative processes, methods of effective communication with policymakers, and organizing community events. By fostering environments where participants can discuss their specific apprehensions about Project 2025, these workshops enable meaningful dialogue and create a sense of unity among attendees.

Creating an effective workshop begins with the careful planning of content that resonates with the community's interests and concerns. Mobilizing attendees involves inviting local experts, community leaders, and activists who can provide valuable insights and share experiences. This not only elevates local concerns but also empowers community members by making them feel heard and validated in their struggles. Providing resources like handouts, toolkits, and follow-up activities ensures that the knowledge gained during workshops is retained and applied effectively.

Training participants in advocacy skills is another critical component. Practical sessions should include role-playing scenarios where participants practice engaging with lawmakers, writing impactful letters, and using social media for activism. Developing these skills helps transform ordinary citizens into effective advocates capable of confronting the challenges posed by Project 2025. Furthermore, creating a network of local advocates who can support one another's initiatives fosters a robust community where knowledge and resources are shared continuously, leading to sustained resistance efforts.

Building a Local Action Network is vital for the ongoing exchange of information, collaboration, and fostering inclusive participation among activist groups. A well-structured network allows for quick dissemination of updates, coordination of activities, and pooling of resources. It creates a robust framework that supports both new and seasoned activists, ensuring everyone has access to relevant information and opportunities to contribute. Communication tools like email listservs, group messaging apps, and regular meetings (virtual or in-person) are instrumental in maintaining these networks.

To kickstart building a local action network, begin by mapping out existing community groups, NGOs, and individual activists willing to collaborate. Organize initial meetings to set common goals, establish communication channels, and delegate responsibilities. Ensure that the network remains inclusive by encouraging diverse representation and promoting equal participation regardless of members' backgrounds or experience levels. Regular check-ins and feedback loops help maintain momentum and address any challenges promptly.

Effective Use of Social Media cannot be overstated in today's digitally connected world. Social media platforms offer vast potential for crafting compelling narratives, spreading awareness, and organizing virtual events. To maximize impact, activists must harness these platforms strategically. Creating authentic and relatable content is key; personal stories and testimonials resonate deeply with audiences and humanize the cause. Consistency in messaging and maintaining a recognizable image for the campaign helps build credibility and keep supporters engaged.

Engaging the community through social media involves more than just posting updates. It's about fostering active dialogue. Using features like polls, live Q&A sessions, and interactive posts encourages followers to participate and feel invested in the cause. Hashtags play a significant role in amplifying messages, and developing unique campaign-specific hashtags can significantly boost visibility. Partnering with influencers who align with the movement's values further extends its reach. They can help spread the message to larger audiences, and their endorsement adds legitimacy to the cause.

Visual content, including infographics, photos, and videos, is crucial for capturing attention and conveying messages effectively. Simple yet powerful visuals can explain complex issues succinctly and memorably. Live streams and events provide real-time interaction opportunities, making the campaign feel immediate and urgent. Whether it's a virtual rally or an educational webinar, these events keep the digital audience engaged and motivated to take further action.

Action-Oriented Petitions and Statements are powerful tools for mobilizing public opinion and exerting pressure on decision-makers. Creating petitions involves clearly defining the issue at hand, articulating specific demands, and gathering signatures from concerned citizens. Online platforms make this process straightforward, enabling broad outreach and ease of signature collection. Public statements serve to inform and rally the community, outlining the stance against Project 2025 and calling for collective action.

Launching a successful petition requires thorough research and consultation with experts to ensure that the demands are feasible and legally sound. Collaborating with legal experts helps in drafting precise language that leaves no room for ambiguity, thus strengthening the petition's impact. Once ready, spreading the petition through social media, email campaigns, and community events ensures maximum visibility and participation.

In addition to the signature collection, follow-up actions like presenting the petition to lawmakers, organizing public demonstrations, and using media coverage to highlight the issue enhance the effectiveness of petitions. Public statements, when crafted strategically, can serve as rallying cries that inspire widespread support. These statements should be disseminated across multiple channels to reach diverse audiences, ensuring that as many people as possible are informed and motivated to join the cause.

Building Coalitions Across Diverse Communities

Identifying common goals is the first step in building coalitions among diverse communities to resist Project 2025. By facilitating discussions that uncover overlapping objectives, we can create inclusive platforms that bring together voices previously fragmented by geographical, social, or ideological divides. Emphasizing shared values such as democracy and social justice fosters a sense of unity and purpose. For instance, communities concerned with climate change and those focused on racial equity might find common ground in resisting policies that threaten both environmental sustainability and civil rights. These conversations enable coalition members to see beyond their immediate concerns and recognize how collective action can achieve broader, mutually beneficial outcomes.

Diverse representation in leadership roles is crucial for any successful coalition. Ensuring that leadership includes representatives from marginalized communities not only amplifies diverse voices but also promotes equity within the group. This means actively seeking out leaders from various backgrounds who have lived experiences relevant to the issues at hand. Such an approach helps address power imbalances and provides a more holistic view of the challenges and potential solutions. For example, including indigenous leaders in environmental justice movements ensures that traditional ecological knowledge is respected and integrated into advocacy strategies. This diversity in leadership enriches decision-making processes and strengthens the coalition's ability to respond to various aspects of Project 2025 effectively.

Cross-community workshops and events are instrumental in fostering understanding and solidarity among coalition members. Organizing events that bring together individuals from different backgrounds creates opportunities for sharing experiences and discussing potential solutions. These gatherings should focus on promoting dialogue, understanding, and collaboration. Workshops can cover topics such as effective advocacy techniques, storytelling, and conflict resolution. Events like these highlight the diversity within the coalition while emphasizing the common goals that unite the members. They also enable participants to build personal connections and trust, which are essential for long-term collaboration. An example could be a workshop where environmental activists and social justice advocates share their perspectives on how Project 2025's policies impact their respective causes, leading to a unified strategy for resistance.

Leveraging existing organizations is another effective strategy for building coalitions. Collaborating with established groups specializing in social justice issues allows coalitions to extend their outreach, share best practices, and maximize their effectiveness. Many organizations already have frameworks and resources that can be adapted for new coalition efforts. By partnering with these entities, coalitions can benefit from their experience and networks. For instance, human rights organizations with a history of lobbying can provide valuable insights and training in legislative advocacy. Similarly, grassroots movements experienced in community organizing can offer strategies for mobilizing local support. This collaborative approach ensures that efforts are not duplicated and that resources are used efficiently, making the coalition's work more impactful.

Building a local action network is vital for maintaining momentum and ensuring sustained resistance against Project 2025. Coordinating activities and campaigns across different communities can help share the workload and increase visibility. Establishing a centralized online space for discussions and planning tactics facilitates communication and ensures everyone is on the same page. Encouraging diverse groups' participation enriches perspectives and strategies, leading to more innovative and comprehensive approaches to advocacy. This network acts as a backbone for the coalition, providing structure and support for ongoing efforts. It enables rapid response to emerging threats and opportunities, ensuring that the coalition remains agile and adaptive.

Effective coalitions require continuous education and engagement to keep members informed and motivated. Hosting regular educational initiatives, such as webinars and informational meetings, helps sustain engagement and ensures that all members are aware of the latest developments related to Project 2025. These sessions can cover a range of topics, from understanding specific policies to developing new advocacy skills. Providing mental health support and resources is also crucial to prevent burnout among activists. Coalition work can be demanding and stressful, so having systems in place to support members' well-being is essential for long-term sustainability.

Adaptive strategies are necessary for responding to the evolving political landscape and the dynamic nature of Project 2025. Regularly reassessing and adapting strategies based on feedback from community members and changes in the external environment ensures that the coalition remains effective. This might involve shifting focus to new priorities, changing tactics, or exploring innovative methods of advocacy. Engaging in self-reflection and learning from successes and failures helps coalitions refine their approaches and maintain their relevance.

Strategies for Collective Advocacy

To effectively oppose the policies proposed in Project 2025, readers must be equipped with robust tactics for collective advocacy. This section will highlight key strategies including collaborative campaign design, legislative lobbying, public demonstrations, and media engagement.

Collaborative Campaign Design

The essence of any successful advocacy effort lies in creating unified campaigns that echo across different demographics. To achieve this, activists should develop messages that resonate broadly yet maintain their core intent. Effective campaign design requires understanding the cultural, social, and economic contexts of various groups to ensure inclusivity and wide appeal. For instance, a campaign against a harmful environmental policy could tailor its message differently for urban residents concerned about air quality and rural communities dependent on agricultural practices impacted by climate change.

Campaigns should also incorporate visual and digital elements that can capture the audience's attention quickly. Using infographics, videos, and social media posts can enhance the reach and impact of the campaign. These tools not only make the information more accessible but can also create viral moments that amplify the campaign’s message.

Additionally, it's crucial to involve community leaders and influencers who can lend credibility and visibility to the campaign. Their endorsement can bridge gaps between diverse demographic groups, fostering a sense of unity and shared purpose. By aligning campaign messages with the values and concerns of different communities, the overall advocacy effort becomes more cohesive and compelling.

Legislative Lobbying

Lobbying legislators is a vital tactic in influencing policy decisions. Activists need to be trained on how to present data-driven arguments that showcase the tangible impacts of Project 2025's policies. This involves gathering credible data, conducting thorough research, and presenting findings in a clear, concise manner. Training sessions can focus on how to structure effective arguments, prioritize talking points, and anticipate counterarguments.

Building relationships with policymakers is equally important. Regular meetings, personalized communication, and attending public forums where legislators are present can help establish rapport and trust. When legislators view activists as informed, respectful, and persistent constituents, they are more likely to consider their viewpoints seriously.

Moreover, coalition-building among various advocacy groups can amplify lobbying efforts. When multiple organizations present a united front, their collective voice carries more weight. For example, coalitions formed around environmental, social justice, and healthcare issues can work together to demonstrate the broad opposition to Project 2025 and propose alternative policies that are more equitable and sustainable.

Public Demonstrations

Public demonstrations serve as powerful tools to mobilize support, draw public attention, and apply pressure on decision-makers. Organizing peaceful protests and rallies can showcase solidarity and amplify the cause. These events should be meticulously planned to ensure safety, legal compliance, and maximum impact.

Protest organizers should seek permits, coordinate with local authorities, and prepare contingency plans in case of disruptions. Effective demonstrations often involve engaging speakers, including affected individuals, experts, and influential activists, who can articulate the message persuasively. Visuals like banners, signs, and art installations can also enhance the demonstration's visibility and emotional appeal.

Technology can play a crucial role in organizing and promoting public demonstrations. Social media platforms can be used to announce events, mobilize participants, and share live updates. Livestreaming the event allows those who cannot attend in person to participate virtually and increases the overall reach of the demonstration. By ensuring that public demonstrations are well-organized and widely publicized, activists can significantly boost their advocacy efforts.

Media Engagement

Effective media engagement is essential for spreading awareness and shaping public opinion. Activists should craft press releases, conduct interviews, and write op-eds that articulate their stance clearly and convincingly. Media coverage can bring the issue to the forefront of public discourse and put additional pressure on policymakers.

Press releases should be well-written and timely, highlighting the most newsworthy aspects of the advocacy effort. They should include quotes from key stakeholders, succinctly explain the issue, and provide contact information for further inquiries. Ensuring that press releases are picked up by media outlets requires building relationships with journalists and editors who cover relevant beats.

Interviews offer a platform for activists to convey their message directly to the audience. Preparation is key; activists should stay focused on their main points, backed by facts and personal stories that humanize the issue. Engaging narratives can capture the audience's interest and foster empathy.

Writing op-eds allows activists to delve deeper into the complexities of Project 2025 and present well-reasoned arguments against it. Op-eds should be persuasive, fact-based, and tailored to the publication's audience. Highlighting real-life examples, potential consequences and practical alternatives can strengthen the argument.

Using digital media strategically can further enhance traditional media efforts. Creating dedicated websites, blogs, or vlog channels provides additional platforms to disseminate information and engage with supporters. Regular updates, interactive content, and direct responses to followers' queries can maintain momentum and keep the advocacy community informed and active.

Sustaining Long-Term Resistance

Mobilizing Against Project 2025 requires an enduring commitment to action and the adoption of strategic methodologies that sustain resistance over time. The key to maintaining prolonged opposition lies in continuously educating the public, managing resources effectively, supporting activists' mental health, and adapting strategies as circumstances evolve.

Continuous education is paramount in keeping communities informed and engaged with ongoing developments. Implementing educational initiatives can involve organizing regular town halls, webinars, and discussion forums where subject matter experts provide updates on Project 2025's legislative changes and their implications. Informative newsletters, podcasts, and social media channels can also play a vital role in disseminating timely information. By ensuring that citizens remain knowledgeable about the latest political moves, these educational efforts help sustain engagement and foster a well-informed coalition of resistors, ready to take action when needed.

Efficient resource management is another critical component in sustaining long-term resistance. Activist groups must establish systems that allow for the effective allocation of both financial and material resources. This might include setting up dedicated funds to support various initiatives, securing long-term funding through grants and donations, and creating a network of volunteers to share the workload. An important aspect of resource management is transparency; by regularly updating supporters on how resources are used, trust within the community is strengthened. Additionally, leveraging technology to create centralized databases for tracking resources and distributing them where they are needed most ensures that activists have the tools necessary to continue their work without interruption.

The mental health of activists is an often-overlooked aspect of sustained resistance. Activists frequently face high levels of stress and burnout due to the demanding nature of their work. Providing mental health resources and establishing support networks is crucial. Offering access to counseling services, organizing peer support groups, and conducting workshops on stress management can help activists maintain their well-being. These initiatives not only assist individuals in coping with the pressures of activism but also build a supportive community where members look out for one another, thereby enhancing overall resilience.

Adaptive strategies are essential in maintaining the efficacy of resistance efforts over time. As the political landscape shifts, so too must the strategies employed by activists. Regularly reassessing tactics and being open to feedback from community members ensures that approaches remain relevant and effective. This could involve periodic strategy meetings where activists analyze the current situation, identify new challenges, and brainstorm innovative solutions. Utilizing data collected from past actions to refine plans can lead to more impactful campaigns. For instance, if a particular protest method proves successful, it can be replicated or adapted to other contexts. Conversely, less effective tactics can be re-evaluated and improved upon.

To illustrate the importance of continuous education, consider the example of environmental advocacy groups that keep their communities apprised of regulatory changes. These groups often conduct workshops explaining new policies, such as those related to clean energy or wildlife protection, and encourage local participation in government consultations. Similar methods can be applied in resisting Project 2025, where educating citizens about proposed restrictions and enabling them to voice their concerns in public forums can galvanize collective action.

In terms of resource management, a pertinent example is the Black Lives Matter movement, which has excelled in organizing fundraisers, managing donations, and allocating resources to various chapters based on need. By adopting a similar approach, activist groups opposing Project 2025 can ensure that resources are available where they will be most impactful, whether that means funding legal challenges, supporting community outreach programs, or providing logistical support for protests.

Supporting activists' mental health can draw insights from organizations like Amnesty International, which has implemented extensive wellness programs for its staff and volunteers. These programs include access to mental health professionals, regular check-ins, and creating safe spaces for sharing experiences. Building similar frameworks for activists opposed to Project 2025 can mitigate the risk of burnout and help maintain a motivated and healthy team.

The concept of adaptive strategies can be exemplified by the ongoing evolution of campaign tactics in the fight for LGBTQ+ rights. Activists in this arena have continually adjusted their methods in response to new legal challenges and societal shifts. Initially focusing on visibility and acceptance, strategies have evolved to include lobbying for specific legislative changes and using digital platforms to reach broader audiences. Similarly, those resisting Project 2025 must remain flexible, constantly refining their strategies to address new threats and leverage emerging opportunities.

Chapter 18: Legal Challenges and Pathways

Legal challenges and pathways for addressing Project 2025 require a critical examination of existing judicial precedents and strategic litigation approaches. The chapter delves into significant court cases that have historically shaped civil rights, personal freedoms, political transparency, and voting rights in the United States. By analyzing these landmark rulings, we can identify potential legal frameworks to contest elements of Project 2025, demonstrating how historical decisions inform contemporary advocacy.

Throughout this chapter, readers will explore the strategic use of community lawyering, public interest law firms, and amicus briefs as powerful tools for mounting effective legal challenges. The discussion further extends into legislative advocacy and coalition-building, underscoring the importance of proactive and collaborative efforts. By understanding past judicial decisions and employing multifaceted legal strategies, advocates can better navigate the complexities of Project 2025, ensuring robust defense mechanisms against its potential adverse impacts on civil liberties and democratic processes.

Major Court Cases That Could Serve as Precedents

The legal challenges surrounding Project 2025 can be framed through the lens of key historical Supreme Court decisions that have shaped American civil rights and liberties. By examining these cases, we can uncover pathways for contemporary advocacy against Project 2025's anticipated impacts. Unpacking the implications of these landmark rulings will help illustrate how legal precedents can provide a sturdy framework for contesting elements of Project 2025 in court.

Brown v. Board of Education is one such cornerstone case. In 1954, the Supreme Court declared state-sponsored segregation unconstitutional, affirming that "separate but equal" violated the Equal Protection Clause of the Fourteenth Amendment. This decision marked a pivotal shift towards dismantling institutionalized racism. Activists today can draw parallels between the discriminatory policies addressed in Brown and those embedded in Project 2025. For instance, if Project 2025 includes initiatives that segregate or marginalize certain communities, advocates can argue that such measures are inherently unequal and violate constitutional principles. The case underscores the judiciary's role in upholding civil rights and emphasizes the importance of framing legal challenges around equality and justice as mandated by the Constitution.

Similarly, Roe v. Wade demonstrates the power of judicial activism in protecting individual freedoms. Although primarily known for establishing women's right to choose, the debates surrounding Roe underscore how interpretations of the constitution can evolve. In 1973, the Supreme Court ruled that a woman's right to privacy extended to her decision to have an abortion. This recognition of personal autonomy set a precedent for defending various personal freedoms. As Project 2025 aims to impose restrictive policies, especially those affecting bodily autonomy and reproductive rights, Roe v. Wade offers a critical framework. Advocates can leverage this decision to argue for the protection of personal freedoms against governmental overreach, emphasizing that shifting legal interpretations should continue to defend individual rights in the face of changing societal norms.

Citizens United v. Federal Election Commission (FEC) brought attention to the influence of money in politics, highlighting the need for transparency and accountability. This 2010 decision allowed corporations and unions to spend unlimited amounts on political campaigns, asserting that such spending is a form of protected speech under the First Amendment. While controversial, Citizens United underscores the significant role that financial resources play in shaping political landscapes. In the context of Project 2025, which may involve substantial campaign finance issues, this case calls for robust legal strategies advocating for greater transparency and accountability. By reinforcing the argument that unchecked financial influence can undermine democratic processes, proponents can push for reforms ensuring that political and electoral integrity remain intact.

Shelby County v. Holder further illustrates the vulnerabilities within voting rights protections. The 2013 decision dismantled a key provision of the Voting Rights Act of 1965, specifically the preclearance requirement, which mandated federal approval for changes to voting laws in jurisdictions with histories of discrimination (*Effects of Shelby County v. Holder on the Voting Rights Act | Brennan Center for Justice*, 2023). This ruling had immediate and profound effects, leading to the enactment of numerous restrictive voting laws. For example, Texas implemented a stringent voter ID law directly after the ruling, significantly affecting people of color who had previously been shielded by the preclearance process. This case serves as a cautionary tale for Project 2025, emphasizing the need for proactive legal strategies to safeguard electoral integrity. By understanding the detrimental impacts of Shelby County v. Holder, advocates can prepare to defend against similar restrictive measures that might arise under Project 2025.

These landmark cases provide essential frameworks and cautionary examples for contemporary legal battles. They stress the importance of vigilant advocacy and the necessity of leveraging legal precedents to challenge unjust policies. The fight against discriminatory practices, the defense of personal freedoms, the call for political transparency, and the safeguarding of voting rights all find their roots in these historic decisions. By learning from past judicial rulings, advocates can build strong, informed arguments to counteract the potential adverse effects of Project 2025.

Understanding Brown v. Board of Education's emphasis on equality helps frame current arguments against any segregative aspects of Project 2025. The decision reinforces the constitutional mandate for equal treatment and provides a robust foundation for challenging policies that marginalize specific groups. Similarly, the judicial activism seen in Roe v. Wade exemplifies how evolving constitutional interpretations can protect personal freedoms. This flexibility is crucial when facing new forms of governmental overreach that Project 2025 might introduce.

The dynamics highlighted in Citizens United v. FEC underscore the ongoing battle against the outsized influence of money in politics. The decision's implications suggest that without transparency and accountability, democracy falters. This insight is invaluable for addressing Project 2025's potential to exacerbate financial inequalities in political arenas. Lastly, the repercussions of Shelby County v. Holder serve as a stark reminder of the fragility of voting rights. Analyzing this case prepares advocates to preemptively guard against erosions of electoral fairness, ensuring that every citizen's voice is heard.

Strategizing Effective Litigation Approaches

Community Lawyering involves a collaborative approach wherein legal professionals work directly with the affected communities to build stronger cases grounded in the lived experiences and needs of those impacted by Project 2025. This method transcends traditional lawyer-client relationships by fostering a deep sense of trust and collaboration, ensuring that legal strategies are not only legally sound but also resonate with the real-life concerns of the community members. By engaging directly with individuals who face the brunt of Project 2025's policies, activists can create compelling narratives that humanize abstract legal principles. These narratives can be instrumental in court, showcasing the tangible adverse effects of the project on people's lives and garnering judicial empathy.

One practical example of community lawyering is its application in environmental justice cases. Legal professionals working with communities exposed to hazardous waste sites often use this approach to gather testimonies and evidence reflecting the health impacts and deteriorated living conditions faced by residents. Such evidence, rooted in firsthand experiences, can significantly strengthen litigation efforts against corporate or governmental entities responsible for environmental harm.

Utilizing Public Interest Law Firms can significantly amplify the impact of legal battles against Project 2025. These firms specialize in representing causes that align with public interests, often operating on a not-for-profit basis. Their expertise in handling complex legal issues, combined with their substantial resources and broader public profile, makes them formidable allies in challenging entrenched power structures. Public interest law firms bring to the table a wealth of experience in navigating the legal system, which is essential for addressing the multifaceted challenges posed by Project 2025.

For instance, the American Civil Liberties Union (ACLU) has a history of taking on cases that defend individual rights and liberties against governmental overreach. Partnering with such organizations can enhance the credibility and reach of legal campaigns against Project 2025. The involvement of a reputable public interest law firm helps to attract media attention and public support, thereby increasing the pressure on policymakers and judicial bodies to act justly.

Strategic Use of Amicus Briefs is another powerful tool in the arsenal of activists and legal professionals. Amicus curiae, meaning "friend of the court," allows organizations or individuals not directly involved in a case to submit briefs providing additional information or arguments. This can be particularly effective in illustrating the broader social implications of a legal issue, thereby bolstering the primary legal arguments made by the parties in the case.

The value of amicus briefs lies in their ability to present perspectives and data that the primary litigants might not cover extensively. For example, in landmark cases concerning civil rights, numerous advocacy groups often file amicus briefs to highlight historical contexts, sociological research, and policy outcomes observed in other jurisdictions. This expansive viewpoint can be critical in persuading judges to consider the widespread ramifications of their rulings, beyond the immediate parties involved in the litigation.

Legislative Advocacy complements litigation by engaging with the legislative process to create laws that counteract the proposals of Project 2025. While litigation focuses on challenging existing statutes and executive actions in court, legislative advocacy works towards influencing the creation of new laws or the amendment of existing ones. This dual approach ensures a robust defense of rights by tackling the issue from multiple fronts—judicial and legislative.

Effective legislative advocacy entails lobbying, coalition-building, and grassroots mobilization to push for legislative changes. Activists must engage with lawmakers, participate in hearings, and contribute to the drafting of legislation that addresses the harmful aspects of Project 2025. Moreover, building coalitions with other advocacy groups, local governments, and concerned citizens can strengthen these efforts by demonstrating widespread opposition to the project and rallying collective action.

A successful example of legislative advocacy is the campaign for marriage equality in the United States, which combined strategic litigation with efforts to change public opinion and pass supportive laws at the state level. This multi-pronged strategy culminated in the Supreme Court's recognition of same-sex marriage as a constitutional right, showcasing how legislative advocacy can effectively complement judicial efforts.

Mobilizing Grassroots Funding

In the fight against Project 2025, grassroots funding becomes a powerful tool in the arsenal of politically active individuals and advocacy groups. This subpoint underscores the significance of such funding mechanisms, exploring how they can offer a counterbalance to the overwhelming corporate influence prevalent in today's political and legal battles.

One of the primary advantages of grassroots donations is their potential to reduce reliance on corporate funds, ensuring that public interest remains at the forefront of political and legal efforts against Project 2025. Often, corporate donations come with strings attached, implicating the recipient organizations in corporate agendas that may not align with public wellbeing. Grassroots funding, however, originates from ordinary citizens who are invested in community-centric outcomes. By diversifying the sources of financial support, organizations challenging Project 2025 can maintain a focus on the issues that matter most to the general populace without compromising their integrity to corporate interests.

Campaign finance reform is another area that benefits significantly from successful grassroots funding models. The 2010 Supreme Court decision in Citizens United v. FEC unleashed a flood of corporate money into politics, creating an uneven playing field where wealthy entities wield disproportionate influence. Showcasing successful examples of grassroots-funded campaigns can provide compelling evidence for the efficacy of campaign finance reform initiatives. When communities rally together to support candidates or causes with small, individual donations, it illustrates the power of collective action and lends weight to arguments for more stringent regulations on corporate contributions. Such real-world success stories can serve as blueprints for legislators and reform advocates aiming to curb the sway of big money in politics.

Moreover, mobilizing small-scale donations does more than just fill campaign coffers; it increases community involvement and ownership over political and legal challenges. When individuals contribute even modest amounts, they become stakeholders in the cause, fostering a sense of collective responsibility and engagement. This heightened participation can invigorate movements, galvanize broader support, and sustain momentum over time. Community-driven fundraising events, like local rallies and online crowdfunding campaigns, also serve as platforms for raising awareness and educating the public about the stakes involved with Project 2025. This dual role of fundraising and advocacy strengthens the social fabric of resistance movements, embedding them deeper within the communities they aim to protect.

Transparency and accountability in funding methods are crucial for building public trust and demonstrating ethical commitment, which is essential in the battle against formidable foes like Project 2025. Transparent reporting practices, where every dollar received and spent is meticulously documented and accessible to the public, help alleviate concerns surrounding misuse or misallocation of funds. Accountability measures, such as regular financial audits by independent bodies, further reinforce this trust. When people see that their financial contributions are being managed responsibly and ethically, confidence in the organization grows. This trust not only encourages continued financial support but also attracts new donors, amplifying the impact of grassroots movements.

An excellent example of effective grassroots funding can be seen in movements such as Bernie Sanders' presidential campaign, which famously shunned large corporate donations in favor of millions of small-dollar contributions. These campaigns demonstrated the feasibility and power of mobilizing grassroots support on a national scale, providing a blueprint for other movements seeking to challenge entrenched corporate interests. They showcased how a robust base of engaged supporters could translate financial clout into significant political influence, a lesson invaluable to those rallying against Project 2025.

Another instructive case is the success of various environmental organizations that rely heavily on grassroots funding. Groups like the Sierra Club have long tapped into broad networks of small donors passionate about conservation and climate action. Their ability to mobilize financial resources from a committed membership base has enabled them to mount effective legal and policy challenges, despite often going up against well-funded corporate adversaries. These instances underscore the importance of cultivating a dedicated donor base, one energized by clear goals and transparent operations.

Additionally, employing modern digital tools can enhance the efficiency and reach of grassroots funding efforts. Social media platforms and crowdfunding websites allow for rapid dissemination of fundraising appeals and facilitate easy, secure donation processes. This technology-driven approach can exponentially expand the reach of grassroots campaigns, engaging a global audience and garnering support from far beyond traditional geographic boundaries. Digital canvassing can amplify the voices of supporters, create viral moments, and generate substantial funds in short periods, illustrating the transformative power of technology in grassroots advocacy.

Building Coalitions for Broad-Based Support

Forming diverse coalitions to broaden support and strengthen litigation against Project 2025 involves uniting different stakeholders. This strategy is vital in creating a formidable front capable of challenging the project's implications effectively. By bringing together varied perspectives and expertise, diverse coalitions significantly enrich the legal arguments against Project 2025, ensuring that a multitude of viewpoints are considered and articulated in court.

Diverse coalitions contribute to richer legal arguments by incorporating insights from various fields. For instance, environmental experts can highlight the ecological repercussions, while civil rights advocates can underscore potential violations of social justice principles. A coalition comprising economists, scientists, and community leaders, among others, ensures that the opposition to Project 2025 is well-rounded and comprehensive. These multifaceted perspectives make it harder for proponents of Project 2025 to ignore or dismiss the coalition's arguments as they represent broader societal concerns.

Furthermore, collaboration across advocacy groups allows for pooling resources and enhancing strategic planning. Many advocacy groups operate within limited funding and resource constraints. However, by forming coalitions, these groups can share their resources, including legal expertise, research data, and communication tools. This collective approach amplifies their capabilities, enabling them to implement more sophisticated and far-reaching legal strategies. Additionally, pooled resources ensure that the coalition can sustain prolonged litigation efforts, which are often necessary for complex legal battles such as those anticipated against Project 2025.

Pooling resources also fosters better strategic planning. When various groups collaborate, they bring different strategic insights and experiences to the table. This diversity in planning can lead to more innovative and effective approaches to litigation. Advocacy groups with experience in lobbying, public relations, and grassroots mobilization can provide invaluable input on how to shape the narrative around Project 2025 and influence public opinion and legislative outcomes. Such strategic collaboration enhances the overall effectiveness of the coalition's efforts.

United efforts not only enhance strategic planning but also increase visibility and public awareness. A coalition of diverse stakeholders can capture the attention of a wider audience, thereby raising awareness about the issues at stake with Project 2025. Increased visibility can be instrumental in swaying judicial and legislative outcomes. Public opinion often plays a crucial role in legal and political decisions, and a united front with broad-based support can exert significant pressure on policymakers and the judiciary. With heightened public awareness, the coalition can garner more media coverage, potentially influencing judges who are sensitive to public sentiment and legislators who are accountable to their constituents.

Moreover, coalition-building fosters resilience and sustained effort, which are crucial for long-term legal battles. Legal challenges against major projects like Project 2025 are typically protracted and resource-intensive. A diverse coalition can maintain momentum over an extended period by distributing the workload among its members. Different organizations within the coalition can take turns leading various aspects of the litigation, ensuring that no single group becomes overwhelmed. This shared responsibility helps sustain the effort needed for success and mitigates the risk of burnout among activists and legal professionals involved in the fight.

The cohesion and mutual support within a coalition can also strengthen the resolve of its members, bolstering their morale and commitment. Knowing that other organizations and individuals stand ready to support and collaborate reinforces a sense of purpose and determination. This solidarity is essential in overcoming setbacks and challenges that will inevitably arise during long-term legal campaigns. By fostering a sense of community and shared mission, coalition-building ensures that the fight against Project 2025 remains robust and resilient.

In addition to these overarching benefits, there are practical examples demonstrating the power of diverse coalitions in legal challenges. In environmental law, successful cases often involve coalitions of local communities, national nonprofits, academic institutions, and even businesses opposing harmful policies. Such coalitions can present a unified front that articulates the widespread impact of ecological degradation, drawing from extensive scientific research and personal testimonies from affected communities.

Similarly, in civil rights litigation, coalitions of minority groups, labor unions, religious organizations, and advocacy groups have historically achieved significant victories by presenting a united stance against discriminatory practices. These coalitions bring together diverse experiences and priorities, making a compelling case that resonates widely with both the public and the courts.

For instance, when states united as amicus curiae filers in cases before the U.S. Supreme Court, their collective efforts were more likely to result in favorable outcomes, particularly when their coalition was regionally diverse (Canelo, 2019). This demonstrates the tangible benefits that diverse coalitions can bring to legal battles, including those against Project 2025.

To emulate these successes, stakeholders opposing Project 2025 should actively seek to form alliances with a wide range of partners. This involves reaching out to groups with shared interests and complementary expertise, such as environmental NGOs, civil liberties organizations, healthcare advocates, and others. Establishing clear communication channels and mutual goals is critical in ensuring that all voices within the coalition are heard and that efforts are well-coordinated.

Chapter 19: Global Repercussions

Understanding the global repercussions of domestic policies is crucial in today's interconnected world. The chapter delves deeply into the international implications of Project 2025, shedding light on how such an initiative could fundamentally alter U.S. foreign policy and its role in global environmental initiatives. By examining the shift towards isolationism and increased unilateral actions, this chapter highlights potential shifts in America's engagement with traditional allies and international agreements. It also discusses the broader impacts these changes may have on global stability, trade dynamics, and multilateral cooperation.

The content of this chapter meticulously explores several dimensions of the topic. It addresses how Project 2025's policies might provoke a departure from multilateral engagements and weaken the U.S.'s advocacy for human rights and democracy abroad. An in-depth analysis is provided on the repercussions of altered trade policies and diminished U.S. involvement in global environmental efforts. Furthermore, the chapter considers the potential for escalated conflicts due to a pivot towards unilateral military action, as well as the long-term consequences for international peacekeeping and diplomatic efforts. This comprehensive examination aims to provide readers with a nuanced understanding of the far-reaching effects that domestic projects can have on the global stage.

Alterations in Foreign Policy and International Relations

Project 2025 heralds a paradigm shift in U.S. foreign policy, one that could profoundly reshape America's global engagements and power dynamics. This subpoint delves into the potential ramifications of the project's policies on international relations, particularly highlighting how these changes might manifest through isolationist tendencies, increased unilateral military actions, compromised advocacy for human rights and democracy, and altered trade policies.

To begin with, Project 2025's inclination towards isolationism could lead to the U.S. stepping back from numerous international agreements and collaborative efforts. Historically, the U.S. has played a pivotal role in fostering multilateral cooperation across various domains, including climate change, security alliances, and economic partnerships. However, an isolationist stance under Project 2025 would signify a dramatic departure from this tradition. The withdrawal from established treaties and pacts not only weakens global governance frameworks but also sends a message to the world that the U.S. is retreating from its leadership role. This may embolden other nations to follow suit, potentially leading to a fragmented international order where collective action becomes exceedingly difficult.

Furthermore, there is a significant risk associated with the potential increase in unilateral military actions under Project 2025. Such a move away from diplomacy towards a more militaristic approach can escalate conflicts in critical regions. An example of this could be heightened tensions in the Middle East, where the U.S. acting independently without coalition support might provoke retaliatory measures from regional powers, exacerbating instability. The legacy of past interventions, such as the invasions of Iraq and Afghanistan, serves as a cautionary tale about the dangers of unilateral military ventures. The resultant prolonged conflicts not only strain U.S. resources but also foster anti-American sentiment, complicating future diplomatic endeavors.

Moreover, Project 2025 could severely hamper the U.S.'s ability to advocate for human rights and democracy abroad. Traditionally, American foreign policy has included a strong emphasis on promoting democratic values and holding foreign governments accountable for human rights violations. However, a more inward-focused administration might deprioritize these efforts. This could reduce pressure on autocratic regimes, thereby enabling them to act with impunity. For instance, countries with poor human rights records might feel less compelled to improve their practices if they perceive diminished scrutiny from the U.S. The broader implications of this could be a weakening of international human rights frameworks and a decline in global democratic norms.

Altered trade policies under Project 2025 present another avenue for significant shifts in U.S. foreign policy. Changes aimed at protecting domestic industries might manifest in increased tariffs and trade barriers, disrupting economic ties with key partners. These protectionist measures could spark retaliatory tariffs from other nations, leading to trade wars that harm U.S. businesses and consumers. For example, American farmers and manufacturers who rely on exports could find themselves facing substantial losses due to reduced market access. Additionally, consumers might face higher prices for goods previously imported tariff-free. Such disruptions can have cascading effects on the global economy, potentially triggering broader economic downturns.

US Standing in Global Environmental Efforts

The policies proposed in Project 2025 could have far-reaching consequences for U.S. leadership in global environmental initiatives and may spark significant international backlash. One of the most striking potential outcomes is the possible exit of the United States from key climate accords, such as the Paris Agreement. This move would not only undermine collective global efforts to reduce greenhouse gas emissions but also signal a retreat from international cooperation on climate change. The withdrawal could have a cascading effect, encouraging other nations to follow suit or reconsider their commitments. Global greenhouse gas emissions might increase as a result, since the absence of the U.S., one of the world's largest emitters, would create a substantial gap in the accord's effectiveness.

Moreover, Project 2025's proposed budget cuts for international climate aid could severely impact support for vulnerable nations facing climate change challenges. The Green Climate Fund intended to help developing countries cope with climate impacts, relies heavily on contributions from developed nations like the U.S. Slashing funding for such initiatives would leave these countries without the essential resources needed to implement mitigation and adaptation strategies. The loss of U.S. financial support would likely exacerbate existing inequalities, making it even harder for these nations to address climatic threats and increasing their reliance on less sustainable practices. This, in turn, would contribute to greater global instability and migration issues as communities become uninhabitable due to climate-induced disasters.

Domestic deregulation under Project 2025 could also hinder the U.S.'s ability to promote effective environmental standards abroad. Environmental regulations often set a benchmark for international norms and practices. When a leading nation like the U.S. rolls back its environmental protections, it sends a message that economic growth takes precedence over ecological well-being. Such deregulation can weaken the country's credibility and diplomatic leverage in advocating for stringent global environmental policies. Without strong domestic regulations, the U.S. would struggle to lead by example, reducing its influence in international forums focused on sustainable development and climate action.

The response of grassroots movements abroad to these policy shifts could further complicate the situation. Activists and organizations outside the U.S. who have traditionally looked up to American leadership in combating climate change may feel betrayed. This sense of abandonment could galvanize them to push for stronger international commitments, independent of U.S. leadership. Movements in Europe, Asia, and Africa might rise in defiance, demanding more ambitious targets from their governments to offset the perceived lack of commitment from the U.S. They could form new coalitions and partnerships aimed at bypassing traditional power structures, thereby reshaping the global environmental movement in unforeseen ways.

Diminished US Engagement and Global Stability

Diminished U.S. engagement on the global stage, resulting from Project 2025, carries significant consequences for global stability and peacekeeping efforts. One major repercussion is the risk of alienating traditional allies while emboldening authoritarian regimes around the world. Historically, the U.S. has upheld alliances through mutual commitments to democratic values and collective security. However, a move towards isolationism could disrupt these long-standing relationships, causing allies to lose confidence in U.S. reliability. When the U.S. steps back, authoritarian regimes may interpret this as an opportunity to expand their influence unchallenged. These regimes thrive when they perceive gaps in the global power structure, seizing chances to assert dominance by exploiting weakened international oversight.

Unilateral military actions under Project 2025 could further escalate conflicts in critical regions. The pivot from multilateral coalitions to solo operations intensifies instability, as it disregards the nuanced dynamics that broad-based diplomatic discussions typically address. For example, without the consensus and shared intelligence that comes with collaborative military strategies, unilateral actions risk miscalculations that can provoke larger conflicts. This approach not only undermines regional stability but also places U.S. forces at greater risk, as the lack of allied support diminishes strategic depth and flexibility. Escalation in such hotspots can lead to prolonged conflicts, drawing in more nations and complicating resolution efforts.

Prioritizing military solutions over diplomatic ones weakens global conflict resolution mechanisms. Diplomacy has always played a crucial role in mitigating tensions and fostering dialogue among conflicting parties. By sidelining diplomacy in favor of military interventions, the U.S. decreases opportunities for peaceful negotiations and sustainable resolutions. Diplomatic channels enable the de-escalation of potential crises before they turn violent, building trust and collaboration among nations. Without robust diplomatic engagement, efforts to resolve conflicts peacefully are significantly impaired, leading to a cycle where military responses become the default rather than the exception. This shift can exacerbate tensions, creating a more volatile international environment and straining resources dedicated to peacekeeping.

The implications for global trade are equally profound as the U.S. retreats from multilateral agreements. Multilateral trade accords rely on the participation and cooperation of multiple countries to establish stable economic relationships and fair trade practices. A U.S. withdrawal could unravel these agreements, leading to a fragmented trade environment susceptible to disputes and protectionist policies. Trade wars could emerge as countries impose tariffs and retaliatory measures, disrupting supply chains and impacting global markets. Such economic discord can harm U.S. businesses and consumers, driving up costs and reducing market access for American products. Moreover, the uncertainty in global trade can stymie economic growth worldwide, affecting both developed and developing economies.

To understand these repercussions fully, it's essential to recognize the interdependence of modern international relations. The U.S. has historically been a pivotal player in shaping the global order, advocating for democratic values, economic cooperation, and collective security. Any substantial change in its engagement strategy reverberates through the global system, influencing how other nations interact with one another. For instance, (the US Department of State, 2022) emphasizes that fragility in regions around the world presents opportunities for violent extremists and criminal organizations to flourish, exploiting governance gaps to further their agendas. Without U.S. leadership in stabilizing these regions, fragile states may become breeding grounds for terrorism, drug trafficking, and other transnational threats that pose direct risks to U.S. interests.

Furthermore, diminished U.S. engagement compromises its ability to build and sustain coalitions necessary for effective peacekeeping. Peacekeeping missions often depend on the contributions and logistical support provided by multiple nations coordinated under a common mandate. According to (Albrecht et al., 2024), peacekeeping efforts reflect a complex assemblage of cooperating entities, each bringing unique capabilities and perspectives. Reducing U.S. involvement would mean losing a significant source of funding, manpower, and strategic direction, which could undermine the operational effectiveness of these missions. The resultant vacuum might see reduced troop commitments from other nations, lessened oversight, and fragmentation of objectives, ultimately diminishing the success rates of peacekeeping endeavors.

This analysis underscores the interconnectedness of military, economic, and diplomatic spheres and how shifts in one area influence broader global dynamics. Alienating allies, escalating conflicts, undermining diplomatic efforts, and provoking trade wars are interlinked consequences of diminished U.S. engagement. To mitigate these risks, a balanced approach incorporating diplomatic, military, and economic strategies is paramount. Maintaining strong alliances and participating in multilateral frameworks ensures that the U.S. continues to play a constructive role in global stability. Collaborative efforts in peacekeeping, conflict resolution, and trade foster a resilient international order capable of addressing contemporary challenges.

Impact on Human Rights and Democratic Movements

Project 2025 represents a significant paradigm shift in U.S. domestic policy, with broad implications for its foreign affairs endeavors, particularly in the realm of human rights and democracy advocacy abroad. By consolidating power within the executive branch, Project 2025 could dramatically hinder U.S. efforts to promote these values on the international stage.

One of the most pressing concerns is the likelihood of reduced accountability for foreign governments concerning human rights violations. Project 2025's proposals include measures that centralize power in the hands of the president, effectively undermining the independence of critical oversight agencies like the Department of Justice (DOJ) and the Federal Bureau of Investigation (FBI). Without these independent bodies maintaining checks and balances, the U.S. will be less inclined or able to hold other nations accountable for human rights abuses. This reduction in pressure can lead to an increase in violations worldwide, as foreign governments may feel emboldened by the lack of consequences from one of the world's leading democratic nations (Radosevich et al., 2024).

Additionally, countries reliant on U.S. support for their democratic movements might experience severe backlash. Historically, American assistance has been crucial for grassroots democratic initiatives across various regions. However, under Project 2025, the U.S. may withdraw or significantly reduce this support due to a shift in priorities toward domestic consolidation of power. As a result, fledgling democracies and movements advocating for democratic reforms might struggle to sustain themselves. The perception that the U.S. no longer supports these democratic ideals may empower authoritarian leaders to crack down harder on dissent, knowing there is a reduced likelihood of international intervention or condemnation (Unmasking the Anti-Democracy Agenda of Project 2025, 2024).

Furthermore, Project 2025 could undermine global human rights frameworks historically led by U.S. leadership. These frameworks, established and maintained through multilateral agreements and institutions like the United Nations Human Rights Council, rely heavily on the commitment and influence of powerful nations like the U.S. With Project 2025 prioritizing domestic policies over international engagement, America's role as a champion of human rights could diminish. Without strong participation from the U.S., these international frameworks may weaken, leading to less coordinated and effective global responses to human rights issues (Unmasking the Anti-Democracy Agenda of Project 2025, 2024).

In light of these potential setbacks, global activists might need to advocate more vigorously for stronger international commitments to counteract U.S. retrenchment. Activists and organizations must leverage the momentum and solidarity built over years of collaboration to pressure other nations into taking the mantle of human rights leadership. This could involve rallying support for international human rights treaties and agreements and holding accountable those who fail to abide by these standards. Grassroots activism and international coalitions will become increasingly crucial to fill the void left by a potentially inward-looking America.

Chapter 20: Empowering Future Generations

Empowering future generations involves integrating American youth into civic engagement initiatives and educational programs that promote critical thinking and activism. This chapter explores how engaging young people in community service projects, youth councils, voter registration drives, and mentorship programs fosters a sense of responsibility and agency. By participating in these activities, youth become aware of social justice issues, understand the significance of their role in society, and develop essential skills for active citizenship. These experiences help bridge the gap between theoretical knowledge and practical application, making abstract concepts like democracy and social equity more tangible and meaningful.

As we delve deeper, this chapter will discuss various methods to involve youth in civic activities, such as community service projects that address local needs and injustice, youth councils that give them a voice in governance, and voter registration drives that emphasize the importance of democratic participation. Additionally, it highlights the value of mentorship programs in guiding at-risk youth toward effective advocacy and activism. By empowering young individuals through these initiatives, we can cultivate a generation of informed, engaged citizens ready to contribute positively to their communities and beyond.

Integrating Youth into Civic Engagement Initiatives

Engaging American youth in civic activities is crucial for fostering a sense of responsibility and agency in shaping their communities. By participating in community service projects, joining youth councils and advisory boards, driving voter registration initiatives, and connecting with mentors, young people not only develop critical skills but also understand the significance of their role in society.

Community service projects are an excellent starting point for involving youth in civic activities. These projects allow young individuals to connect directly with their community's needs and contribute to addressing social justice issues. For example, organizing a neighborhood clean-up can help them recognize environmental injustices and the importance of a sustainable environment. Additionally, volunteering at local shelters or food banks exposes them to the plights of underserved populations and instills a sense of compassion and empathy. Such experiences bridge the gap between theory and practice, making abstract concepts like social justice more tangible. A guideline here is to ensure that these projects align with the interests and strengths of the participants, making the experience both educational and fulfilling.

Youth councils and advisory boards offer another vital platform for engagement. These bodies give young people a say in local governance, allowing them to influence decisions that affect their lives. By participating, they develop leadership skills, learn the intricacies of policymaking, and understand the value of informed citizenship. For instance, a high school student serving on a city's parks and recreation board may provide unique insights into the creation of spaces that cater to younger demographics. This hands-on involvement encourages them to take ownership of their community's future. To maximize the effectiveness of youth councils, it's essential to provide adequate training and support, ensuring that young voices are heard and respected in decision-making processes.

Voter registration drives are pivotal in empowering young people to participate in democracy. Understanding the voting process demystifies political engagement and underscores its significance. Education on voter rights and the electoral process can transform passive observers into active participants in democratic governance. For example, students can organize campus-based registration tables, making it convenient for peers to register and emphasizing the importance of each vote. Mobilization efforts like these not only increase voter turnout but also foster a culture of political involvement from a young age. A practical guideline here is to incorporate real-life simulations or mock elections within educational settings to provide firsthand experience of the voting process.

Mentorship programs play a critical role, especially for at-risk youth, by connecting them with mentors who have experience in civic and political spaces. These relationships provide guidance, knowledge, and networking opportunities that might otherwise be inaccessible. For instance, a mentor who has experience in community organizing can introduce mentees to strategies for effective advocacy and activism. Mentors can also help navigate the complexities of civic duties, offering advice and support that builds confidence and competence. A successful mentorship program requires careful matching of mentors and mentees based on interests and goals, regular check-ins, and creating opportunities for meaningful engagement.

Curriculum Reform

Advocating for educational systems to include social justice and civic education in their core curriculum can transform the landscape of American education. Integrating these subjects into the educational framework is critical to prepare future generations to engage thoughtfully and constructively with societal structures. This subpoint explores the immense value these subjects bring, emphasizing not only knowledge acquisition but also the cultivation of practical skills essential for active participation in democracy.

Incorporating social justice and civic education equips students with the knowledge necessary to critically analyze societal structures. Understanding historical and contemporary issues related to justice, equity, and governance empowers students to identify systemic inequalities and consider solutions grounded in fairness and inclusivity. This kind of education does not merely impart facts—it encourages analytical thinking, fostering a generation that approaches problems with a critical eye and an informed perspective. Civic education, in particular, provides an understanding of governmental processes, political ideologies, and constitutional rights, enabling students to navigate and challenge political landscapes effectively (Winthrop, 2020).

The necessity of curriculum reform is evident in its potential to cultivate an informed electorate ready to tackle contemporary challenges. By integrating civic education from elementary through high school, students develop a robust understanding of public issues and civic responsibilities. Early exposure ensures that by the time they are eligible to vote, they possess the knowledge and confidence to engage meaningfully in democratic processes. A reformed curriculum that prioritizes these areas is not just beneficial—it is indispensable in creating citizens who are well-versed in public discourse and capable of contributing to the betterment of society.

Practical skills alongside theoretical knowledge are crucial in fostering activism from a young age. Experiential learning methods such as service-learning projects and extracurricular activities provide hands-on opportunities for students to apply classroom lessons to real-world situations. These experiences solidify theoretical knowledge by demonstrating its relevance and application in everyday life. For instance, participating in community service or school governance teaches students about collaboration, leadership, and civic responsibility. It instills a sense of agency, showing them that they can influence change within their communities.

Moreover, exposure to social justice topics instills a lifelong commitment to civic engagement. When students regularly explore issues of equity and justice, it shapes their worldview and ethical framework. They learn to appreciate the importance of advocating for marginalized groups and understand the impact of systemic inequalities. Equipped with this understanding, they are more likely to pursue careers and lifestyles dedicated to promoting justice and equity. Studies have shown that students exposed to comprehensive civic education demonstrate higher levels of civic engagement, including voting, volunteering, and attending public meetings (Winthrop, 2020).

Curriculum reform is pivotal in achieving these outcomes. Schools must adopt holistic approaches that integrate social justice and civic topics within various subjects rather than treating them as standalone units. This integration requires carefully designed curricula that address both the cognitive and affective dimensions of learning. Educators should be provided with adequate training and resources to deliver these subjects effectively, ensuring that they can foster a balanced understanding of complex issues among their students. Active discussions, debates, and critical reflections should be routine practices in classrooms to encourage diverse viewpoints and constructive dialogue.

Additionally, the role of schools extends beyond classroom instruction. Educational institutions can model civic values by being inclusive spaces where community members connect and collaborate. Schools in areas with limited civic engagement opportunities can become hubs for community activities, thereby demonstrating the principles of civic participation. When students see their schools embodying the values they learn about, it reinforces the importance and feasibility of civic engagement in their lives.

Social justice education, when implemented correctly, avoids ideological indoctrination and instead fosters independent thinking and analytical skills. Critics often argue that teaching social justice in schools pushes a politically correct agenda; however, effective social justice education presents multiple perspectives on issues, allowing students to form their own informed opinions (Soken-Huberty, 2020). Teachers play a crucial role in this process by encouraging debate, presenting current events, and helping students make connections between historical contexts and contemporary issues. This approach nurtures an environment where students learn to respect differing viewpoints and develop their understanding through evidence-based reasoning.

The benefits of integrating social justice and civic education into the core curriculum extend far beyond individual student development. As students grow into adults who value equity and civic responsibility, they contribute to a society that is more just and democratic. An informed and engaged citizenry is essential in addressing the pressing challenges of modern society, from climate change to social inequalities. By laying the groundwork for critical thinking and active participation, educational systems can ensure that future generations are equipped to lead with integrity and purpose.

Debate and Public Speaking Programs

Empowering youth to articulate their views effectively through debate and public speaking programs is crucial in shaping active and informed citizens. These programs equip young people with the skills necessary to communicate their thoughts, advocate for issues they care about, and engage meaningfully in democratic processes.

First, developing communication skills allows young people to advocate for issues they care about. When students engage in public speaking or debate, they learn how to research topics, organize their thoughts, and present arguments logically and persuasively. This is particularly important when addressing social issues or policy changes that directly impact their communities. For instance, a high school student passionate about climate change might participate in a debate on environmental policies, learning to use evidence-based arguments to advocate for greener practices. Effective communication thus transforms personal passion into actionable advocacy, enabling youth to take an active role in societal discourse.

Participation in debates fosters critical thinking and helps youth navigate diverse perspectives. In debates, students are often required to argue both sides of an issue, which encourages them to consider multiple viewpoints and understand the complexity of real-world problems. This process enhances their ability to think critically, identify logical fallacies, and synthesize information from various sources. For example, debating the merits and drawbacks of universal healthcare can help students appreciate the economic, ethical, and practical dimensions of the topic. As they refine their arguments, they also develop better listening skills, learning to respond thoughtfully to opposing viewpoints and build on their ideas.

Such programs enhance self-confidence, encouraging young people to voice their opinions in public forums. Overcoming stage fright and nervousness is a significant aspect of public speaking training. Regular practice and constructive feedback help students grow more comfortable speaking in front of others, gradually building their confidence. This newfound self-assurance extends beyond the classroom, preparing them for future challenges in college, job interviews, and community leadership roles. Moreover, receiving positive reinforcement from peers and mentors can further boost their self-esteem, making them more willing to share their ideas and participate actively in discussions.

These skills are crucial for engaging in meaningful discussions and influencing policy decisions. In today's polarized political climate, the ability to debate respectfully and constructively is more important than ever. Public speaking and debate programs teach students how to frame their arguments in ways that resonate with different audiences, fostering respectful dialogue even in contentious situations. By articulating their views clearly and confidently, young people can influence public opinion, contribute to policy debates, and drive social change. For instance, a well-prepared speech at a town hall meeting can sway local officials' opinions on youth-related issues such as education reform or mental health services.

Moreover, these programs provide invaluable life skills that extend into professional environments. Effective communication is essential in nearly all careers, whether presenting a project proposal, negotiating with colleagues, or leading a team. Public speaking experience also makes individuals more persuasive and confident in professional settings, enhancing their overall employability. Many employers prioritize strong communication skills when hiring, recognizing that employees who can express ideas clearly and engage constructively with others are valuable assets to any organization.

A key benefit of these programs is the development of leadership and management skills. Leaders must be able to communicate their vision, inspire their teams, and navigate complex negotiations. Debate and public speaking activities inherently foster these abilities, as students learn to structure their arguments, persuade audiences, and handle pressure. Through these experiences, they develop the resilience and adaptability necessary for effective leadership. Additionally, engaging in these programs often involves teamwork, where students collaborate, share responsibilities, and support one another's growth.

By participating in debate and public speaking activities, students also become more aware of current events and societal issues. Researching various topics for speeches or debates requires them to stay informed about national and global affairs, broadening their understanding of the world. This knowledge empowers them to participate in civic activities with greater context and insight, making their contributions more impactful. For example, understanding the nuances of immigration policy can enable a student to advocate more effectively for humane and just reforms.

Finally, enhanced communication skills facilitate better interaction within the community. Youth who are confident speakers are more likely to engage in community service projects, join local organizations, and take part in civic initiatives. Their ability to articulate their views and listen actively to others helps build stronger, more connected communities. For instance, a young person leading a community workshop on recycling can educate others, mobilize action, and foster a sense of collective responsibility.

Workshops on Media Literacy

In today's digital age, the rapid proliferation of information demands that we equip our youth with the skills to navigate this complex landscape. Teaching students how to critically evaluate information sources through media literacy workshops is paramount in empowering them to become discerning consumers of media.

Equipping Youth with Media Literacy Skills

At its core, media literacy involves the ability to access, analyze, and evaluate media in multiple forms. By fostering these skills in youth, we enable them to identify misinformation and advocate for truth in media. Young people are constantly bombarded with content from a variety of sources, many of which may present biased or false information. Through structured media literacy workshops, students learn to question the reliability and intentions behind the information they consume.

For example, imagine a high school student scrolling through their social media feed. They come across an article with a sensational headline designed to provoke an emotional response. Instead of taking it at face value, the student applies the critical thinking skills they've acquired from their media literacy training. They investigate the source, cross-check facts with reputable outlets, and evaluate the biases that might be present. This process not only helps them discern credible information but also reduces their likelihood of sharing misleading content (Patel, 2024).

Understanding Media Dynamics

An informed citizenry is essential for a functioning democracy. Understanding media dynamics equips young individuals to challenge authoritarian narratives. Authoritarian regimes often manipulate media to control public perception and stifle dissent. By contrast, a population well-versed in media literacy can recognize such manipulations and resist propagandist tactics.

Consider the recent rise of deepfake technology, which can create convincing yet entirely fabricated video and audio content. Without media literacy training, this could easily deceive large segments of the population. However, educated youth who understand the existence and potential misuse of such technology are better prepared to question and verify the authenticity of what they see and hear, ultimately challenging false narratives and demanding accountability from those in power.

Skillful Analysis of News

The ability to skillfully analyze news fosters engagement in critical discussions about the political climate and individual choices. When students can dissect news stories, identify underlying biases, and understand the broader context, they become active participants in democratic processes. This analytical skill is particularly important during election cycles when political rhetoric can be highly charged and polarizing.

For instance, a student trained in media literacy may engage in a classroom debate about a current political issue. Equipped with the skills to differentiate between fact-based reporting and opinion pieces, they contribute thoughtfully to the discussion, presenting well-researched arguments and challenging unsupported claims made by peers. This kind of engagement not only enhances their understanding of political issues but also encourages a more thoughtful and informed electorate (Schulten, 2022).

Empowering Informed Decision-Making

Media literacy is vital for empowering youth to make informed decisions and contribute to a healthy democracy. Informed decision-making extends beyond political choices; it encompasses daily interactions, from consumer behavior to social relationships. By understanding the influence of media, young people can make better decisions that align with their values and promote societal well-being.

For example, consider the impact of advertising on teenage consumer habits. Without media literacy skills, teenagers might be more susceptible to marketing ploys that encourage unhealthy eating habits or unrealistic body images. A media literacy workshop that teaches students to analyze and deconstruct advertising messages enables them to recognize persuasive techniques and make healthier lifestyle choices.

Integrating Media Literacy into Educational Systems

To ensure that media literacy becomes an integral part of education, effective strategies for its integration must be implemented. Schools can incorporate media literacy into existing curricula, ensuring that all students receive consistent instruction across grade levels. Collaboration with libraries and community organizations can further enhance these efforts, providing additional resources and real-world applications.

Workshops can take various forms, from analyzing news articles and social media posts to creating media projects that highlight the importance of accurate information. These hands-on activities make learning engaging and relevant, helping students apply their skills in practical ways. Additionally, educators should receive professional development to effectively teach media literacy, and stay updated on the latest trends and technologies.

Overcoming Challenges

Integrating media literacy into educational systems is not without challenges. One major hurdle is ensuring equitable access to these programs, especially in underserved communities where technology and resources may be limited. Addressing this gap requires concerted efforts from policymakers, educators, and community leaders to provide the necessary infrastructure and support.

Another challenge is keeping pace with the rapidly evolving media landscape. As new platforms and technologies emerge, media literacy curricula must adapt accordingly. Continuous research and collaboration with experts in the field can help educators stay ahead of these changes, ensuring that students are prepared to navigate the digital world successfully.

Conclusion

As we draw this journey to a close, it is crucial to reflect on the major themes that have anchored our exploration of Project 2025 and its profound implications for American society. Throughout these chapters, we have delved deeply into the numerous ways in which Project 2025 threatens our democracy, erodes civil liberties, and undermines social equity. From the restrictions on personal freedoms analyzed in Chapter 5, to the endangerment of essential social programs discussed in Chapter 14, we have seen how this blueprint caters primarily to the interests of the elite while disregarding the needs and voices of everyday Americans.

One of the overarching themes has been the risk posed by authoritarian tendencies embedded within Project 2025. In an era where democratic norms are increasingly under siege, understanding these threats becomes more crucial than ever. The policies proposed within this project are not just abstract ideas but concrete plans with the potential to reshape the political landscape drastically. They pave the way for a future where power is centralized, dissent is stifled, and the rich-poor divide widens further.

Equally alarming are the implications for civil liberties. We have examined how Project 2025 seeks to curtail freedoms that many of us take for granted—freedom of speech, the right to privacy, and the right to protest among others. These rights are foundational pillars of any functioning democracy. Their erosion could lead to a society where critical voices are silenced, and governmental overreach becomes the norm.

Social equity, another critical theme, has also been placed at the forefront of our discussions. Marginalized communities—already vulnerable under the current system—stand to suffer disproportionately from the implementation of Project 2025. Whether it's through cuts to social welfare programs, environmental deregulations that poison low-income neighborhoods, or policies that amplify systemic racism, the repercussions are widespread and devastating.

Armed with this knowledge, it's important to remember that awareness is the first step towards activism. This book is not just a narrative but a call to arms for anyone concerned about the direction in which our nation is heading. Now that you have a comprehensive understanding of what Project 2025 entails, you possess the tools to engage in meaningful dialogue and mobilize your community. Whether it's attending local council meetings, participating in peaceful protests, or simply having informed conversations with friends and family, your actions can contribute significantly to the broader resistance against authoritarianism.

Empowerment comes not just from understanding but from taking action. Awareness without activism is akin to knowing the path but refusing to walk it. By disseminating the insights you've gained, you can help build a collective consciousness aimed at safeguarding democratic principles. Every conversation, every vote, every petition signed adds up to a more robust defense against the encroaching tide of authoritarian rule.

Moreover, this empowerment should not be confined to immediate actions alone but should extend to inspiring future generations. The responsibility lies with all of us to educate the young minds who will inherit the political framework of tomorrow. Instilling values of justice, equality, and democracy in our youth ensures that the fight for a fair and equitable society continues long after we're gone. It is through them that our ideals will be perpetuated, and our efforts will bear fruit.

Imagine an America where young leaders are equipped with both the historical context and the moral fortitude to challenge injustices. An America where the lessons learned from the struggles against Project 2025 serve as a guidebook for navigating future threats to democracy. By nurturing such a generation, we do more than resist present dangers—we build a resilient society capable of withstanding challenges yet to come.

In conclusion, the journey through this book has been one of clarity, urgency, and hope. Clarity in understanding the multifaceted threats posed by Project 2025; urgency in recognizing the need for immediate action; and hope in the realization that empowered citizens can indeed make a difference. The stakes are high, but so too is our collective potential to effect change.

Our democracy, civil liberties, and social equity are not guaranteed—they require vigilant protection and proactive stewardship. As individuals committed to these ideals, your role extends beyond mere acknowledgment of the problems. It involves rolling up your sleeves and engaging in the relentless pursuit of a more just and equitable society.

May the insights you've gained serve as both a warning and a beacon—a warning of the dangers that lie in complacency and a beacon guiding your efforts toward meaningful participation in democratic processes. The story doesn't end here; it merely turns a page. As you step into the next chapter of activism and advocacy, know that your contributions, however small they may seem, are vital threads in the fabric of our nation's future.

Thank you for embarking on this journey. Let it empower you, inspire you, and drive you to take action. Together, we can ensure that democracy not only survives but thrives for generations to come.

Reference List

Berman, G. (2024, August 13). *"It's time to be very afraid": Discussing political violence*. The Fulcrum; The Fulcrum. https://thefulcrum.us/bridging-common-ground/political-violence-2389075

Coan, J. (2024, June 18). *To save America, add trust and subtract polarizing words*. The Fulcrum; The Fulcrum. https://thefulcrum.us/bridging-common-ground/building-trust-among-americans

Cohen, M. (2024, June 28). *What Is Project 2025 and Why Is It Alarming?* Democracy Docket. https://www.democracydocket.com/analysis/what-is-project-2025-and-why-is-it-alarming/

Project 2025: Democratic Doomsday - Berkeley Political Review. (2023, November 17). https://bpr.studentorg.berkeley.edu/2023/11/17/project-2025-democratic-doomsday/

Rodriguez, C. (2024). *Project 2025: The plan to seize power by gutting America's system of checks and balances. Center for American Progress*. Retrieved from https://www.americanprogress.org/article/project-2025-the-plan-to-seize-power-by-gutting-americas-system-of-checks-and-balances/

Walker, A. (2023). *Project 2025 sparks fear of dictatorship and oppression. The Miami Times*. Retrieved from https://www.miamitimesonline.com/news/latest_reports/project-2025-sparks-fear-of-dictatorship-and-oppression/article_165a1c10-1d14-11ef-94fd-53872b255fa8.html

Allen, J. (2023, October 13). *Social Movements and U.S. Political Parties: Evolutionary and Revolutionary Change*. Protect Democracy. https://protectdemocracy.org/work/social-movements-and-political-parties/

Foundation, T. H. (n.d.). *Solutions 2020 | The Heritage Foundation*. Solutions 2020 | the Heritage Foundation. https://www.heritage.org/solutions/

MSNBC. (2024, July 9). *Unpacking WTH Project 2025 is with Thomas Zimmer: podcast and transcript*. MSNBC.com; MSNBC. https://www.msnbc.com/msnbc-podcast/why-is-this-happening/unpacking-wth-project-2025-thomas-zimmer-podcast-transcript-rcna160927

National Archives. (n.d.). *The Reagan Presidency*. Ronald Reagan Presidential Library and Museum. https://www.reaganlibrary.gov/reagans/reagan-administration/reagan-presidency

Nash, G. (1986, May). *American Conservatives and the Reagan Revolution*. Imprimis. https://imprimis.hillsdale.edu/american-conservatives-and-the-reagan-revolution/

O'Brien, J., & Abdelhadi, E. (2020, April 23). *Re-examining Restructuring: Racialization, Religious Conservatism, and Political Leanings in Contemporary American Life*. Social Forces. https://doi.org/10.1093/sf/soaa029

Repucci, S., & Slipowitz, A. (2022). *The Global Expansion of Authoritarian Rule*. Freedom House. https://freedomhouse.org/report/freedom-world/2022/global-expansion-authoritarian-rule

Storrs, L. R. Y. (2015). *McCarthyism and the Second Red Scare. Oxford Research Encyclopedia of American History*. https://doi.org/10.1093/acrefore/9780199329175.013.6

The Reagan Revolution | US History II (OS Collection). (2019). Lumenlearning.com. https://courses.lumenlearning.com/suny-ushistory2os2xmaster/chapter/the-reagan-revolution/

Albert, Z. (2024, July 19). *Project 2025 is the latest example of the Heritage Foundation's long history of conservative advocacy*. Chicago Sun-Times; Chicago Sun-Times. https://chicago.suntimes.com/other-views/2024/07/18/project-2025-heritage-foundations-history-conservative-advocacy-zachary-albert-the-conversation

Albert, Z. (2024, July 18). *Heritage Foundation's "Project 2025" is just the latest action plan from a group with an over 50-year history of steering GOP lawmaking*. The Conversation. https://theconversation.com/heritage-foundations-project-2025-is-just-the-latest-action-plan-from-a-group-with-an-over-50-year-history-of-steering-gop-lawmaking-234542

Blitzer, J. (2024, July 15). *Inside the Trump Plan for 2025*. The New Yorker. https://www.newyorker.com/magazine/2024/07/22/inside-the-trump-plan-for-2025

Project 2025, Explained | American Civil Liberties Union. (2024, August 14). American Civil Liberties Union. https://www.aclu.org/project-2025-explained

The conservative think tank behind the controversial Project 2025 faces Trump's ire. (2024, July 20). NPR. https://www.npr.org/2024/07/20/nx-s1-5044495/the-conservative-think-tank-behind-the-controversial-project-2025-faces-trumps-ire

Diamond, L. (2004, February 12). *Why Decentralize Power in A Democracy? | Larry Diamond*. Diamond-Democracy.stanford.edu. https://diamond-democracy.stanford.edu/speaking/speeches/why-decentralize-power-democracy

Rudman, M., DeLeon, R., & Martinez, J. (2021, June 16). *Redefining Homeland Security: A New Framework for DHS To Meet Today's Challenges*. Center for American Progress. https://www.americanprogress.org/article/redefining-homeland-security-new-framework-dhs-meet-todays-challenges/

Romaguera, R. A., & Meenakshi Lakshman. (2023, April 7). *Funding and Accountability in Public Programs: Implications for Disease Intervention Specialists*. Sexually Transmitted Diseases; Lippincott Williams & Wilkins. https://doi.org/10.1097/olq.0000000000001815

Swan, J., Savage, C., & Haberman, M. (2023, July 17). *Trump and Allies Forge Plans to Increase Presidential Power in 2025*. The New York Times. https://www.nytimes.com/2023/07/17/us/politics/trump-plans-2025.html

Tracking regulatory changes in the Biden era. (2024, January 4). Brookings. https://www.brookings.edu/articles/tracking-regulatory-changes-in-the-biden-era/

Vian, T. (2020, February 3). *Anti-corruption, Transparency and Accountability in health: concepts, frameworks, and Approaches*. Global Health Action. https://doi.org/10.1080/16549716.2019.1694744

Wang, D., Wang, L., Wei, S., Yu, P., Sun, H., Jiang, X., & Hu, Y. (2022, May 12). *Effects of Authoritarian Leadership on Employees' Safety Behavior: a Moderated Mediation Model*. Frontiers in Public Health. https://doi.org/10.3389/fpubh.2022.846842

Zamore, M. (2024, August 29). *Project 2025 Offers Dystopian View of America*. American Civil Liberties Union. https://www.aclu.org/news/civil-liberties/project-2025-offers-dystopian-view-of-america

Diamond, L. (2004, February 12). *Why Decentralize Power in A Democracy? | Larry Diamond*. Diamond-Democracy.stanford.edu. https://diamond-democracy.stanford.edu/speaking/speeches/why-decentralize-power-democracy

Rudman, M., DeLeon, R., & Martinez, J. (2021, June 16). *Redefining Homeland Security: A New Framework for DHS To Meet Today's Challenges*. Center for American Progress. https://www.americanprogress.org/article/redefining-homeland-security-new-framework-dhs-meet-todays-challenges/

Romaguera, R. A., & Meenakshi Lakshman. (2023, April 7). *Funding and Accountability in Public Programs: Implications for Disease Intervention Specialists*. Sexually Transmitted Diseases; Lippincott Williams & Wilkins. https://doi.org/10.1097/olq.0000000000001815

Swan, J., Savage, C., & Haberman, M. (2023, July 17). *Trump and Allies Forge Plans to Increase Presidential Power in 2025*. The New York Times. https://www.nytimes.com/2023/07/17/us/politics/trump-plans-2025.html

Tracking regulatory changes in the Biden era. (2024, January 4). Brookings. https://www.brookings.edu/articles/tracking-regulatory-changes-in-the-biden-era/

Vian, T. (2020, February 3). *Anti-corruption, Transparency and Accountability in health: concepts, frameworks, and Approaches*. Global Health Action. https://doi.org/10.1080/16549716.2019.1694744

Wang, D., Wang, L., Wei, S., Yu, P., Sun, H., Jiang, X., & Hu, Y. (2022, May 12). *Effects of Authoritarian Leadership on Employees' Safety Behavior: a Moderated Mediation Model*. Frontiers in Public Health. https://doi.org/10.3389/fpubh.2022.846842

Zamore, M. (2024, August 29). *Project 2025 Offers Dystopian View of America*. American Civil Liberties Union. https://www.aclu.org/news/civil-liberties/project-2025-offers-dystopian-view-of-america

Anderson, J., Rainie, L., & Vogels, E. (2021, February 18). *Experts Say the "New Normal" in 2025 Will Be Far More Tech-Driven, Presenting More Big Challenges*. Pew Research Center. https://www.pewresearch.org/internet/2021/02/18/experts-say-the-new-normal-in-2025-will-be-far-more-tech-driven-presenting-more-big-challenges/

ACLU. (2024, August 28). *Why Kamala Harris Must Break the Cycle of Unlawful and Abusive Government Surveillance | ACLU*. American Civil Liberties Union. https://www.aclu.org/news/civil-liberties/why-kamala-harris-must-break-the-cycle-of-unlawful-and-abusive-government-surveillance

Lai, S., & Tanner, B. (2022, July 18). *Examining the intersection of data privacy and civil rights*. Brookings. https://www.brookings.edu/articles/examining-the-intersection-of-data-privacy-and-civil-rights/

Project 2025 Exposed | GLAAD. (2024, July 9). Glaad.org. https://glaad.org/project-2025/

The Surveillance Gap: The Harms of Extreme Privacy and Data Marginalization. (n.d.). N.Y.U. Review of Law & Social Change. https://socialchangenyu.com/review/the-surveillance-gap-the-harms-of-extreme-privacy-and-data-marginalization/

The Free Expression Project | ACLU Massachusetts. (2023, November 9). Www.aclum.org. https://www.aclum.org/en/free-expression-project

CBPP. (2024). *House republican agendas and Project 2025 would increase poverty and hardship, drive up the uninsured rate, and disinvest people, communities, and the economy. Center on Budget and Policy Priorities*. Retrieved from https://www.cbpp.org/research/federal-budget/house-republican-agendas-and-project-2025-would-increase-poverty-and

Choi, Y. J., Huber, E., Kim, W. S., Kwon, H. Y., & Shi, S.-J. (2020, April 2). *Social investment in the knowledge-based economy: new politics and policies*. Policy and Society. https://doi.org/10.1080/14494035.2020.1782577

Congress Must Bolster Youth Employment Programs To Secure America's Economic Future. (2023, April 24). Center for American Progress. https://www.americanprogress.org/article/congress-must-bolster-youth-employment-programs-to-secure-americas-economic-future/

Kimer, J. (2021, March 31). *The Role of the Private Sector in Catalyzing Inclusive Economic Opportunities in the Northern Triangle*. Atlantic Council. https://www.atlanticcouncil.org/in-depth-research-reports/issue-brief/the-role-of-the-private-sector-in-catalyzing-inclusive-economic-opportunities-in-the-northern-triangle/

Team, F. 11 D. (2024, June 28). *Project 2025 and its potential impact on Americans*. FOX 11. https://www.foxla.com/news/project-2025-its-potential-impact-americans

Vocational and skills training programs to improve labor market outcomes. (n.d.). The Abdul Latif Jameel Poverty Action Lab (J-PAL). https://www.povertyactionlab.org/policy-insight/vocational-and-skills-training-programs-improve-labor-market-outcomes

Budryk, Z., & Frazin, R. (2024). *What Project 2025 would mean for the fight against climate change. The Hill*. Retrieved from https://thehill.com/policy/energy-environment/4769252-project-2025-climate-change-energy-environment/

Environmental Protection Agency. (2019, March 14). *Progress Cleaning the Air and Improving People's Health | US EPA*. United States Environmental Protection Agency. https://www.epa.gov/clean-air-act-overview/progress-cleaning-air-and-improving-peoples-health

Fuller, R. (2022). *Pollution and health: a Progress Update*. The Lancet Planetary Health. https://doi.org/10.1016/S2542-5196(22)00090-0

Simhoni, S. (2024). *How project 2025 threatens the Inflation Reduction Act's thriving clean energy economy. Center for American Progress*. Retrieved from https://www.americanprogress.org/article/how-project-2025-threatens-the-inflation-reduction-acts-thriving-clean-energy-economy/

What Project 2025 Would Mean for Climate Change - Atmos. (2024, July 18). Atmos. https://atmos.earth/what-project-2025-would-mean-for-climate-change/

Young, B. G., Andrea Thompson, Tanya Lewis, Lauren J. (n.d.). *Project 2025's Blueprint for a Second Trump Presidency Spells Out How to Harm U.S. Science*. Scientific American. https://www.scientificamerican.com/article/project-2025-plan-for-trump-presidency-has-far-reaching-threats-to-science/

American University. (2019, July 24). *The Benefits of Inclusion and Diversity in the Classroom | American University*. Soeonline.american.edu. https://soeonline.american.edu/blog/benefits-of-inclusion-and-diversity-in-the-classroom/

Gamage, K. A. A., Dehideniya, D. M. S. C. P. K., & Ekanayake, S. Y. (2021, July 16). *The Role of Personal Values in Learning Approaches and Student Achievements*. Behavioral Sciences. https://www.ncbi.nlm.nih.gov/pmc/articles/PMC8301052/

Intercultural Development Research Association. (2022, November 22). *Classroom Censorship Hurts Students*. IDRA. https://www.idra.org/education_policy/classroom-censorship-hurts-students/

Southall, A. (2022, September 27). *Censorship Is Ruining America's Education | YIP Institute*. Yipinstitute.org. https://yipinstitute.org/capstone/censorship-is-ruining-americas-education

Banerjee, A. (2023, January 18). *The economics of abortion bans*. Economic Policy Institute. https://www.epi.org/publication/economics-of-abortion-bans/

Dehlendorf, C., Rodriguez, M. I., Levy, K., Borrero, S., & Steinauer, J. (2010, March). *Disparities in family planning*. American Journal of Obstetrics and Gynecology. https://doi.org/10.1016/j.ajog.2009.08.022

Expanding Medicaid Can Save Lives. (2019, August 12). California Health Care Foundation. https://www.chcf.org/blog/expanding-medicaid-can-save-lives/

Harker, L. (2024). *Medicaid expansion helps newly eligible adults and groups traditionally eligible for Medicaid. Center on Budget and Policy Priorities*. Retrieved from https://www.cbpp.org/research/health/medicaid-expansion-helps-newly-eligible-adults-and-groups-traditionally-eligible

Loss of the Affordable Care Act Would Widen Racial Disparities in Health Coverage. (2020, October 1). KFF. https://www.kff.org/policy-watch/loss-of-the-affordable-care-act-would-widen-racial-disparities-in-health-coverage/

National Academies of Sciences, E., Division, H. and M., Practice, B. on P. H. and P. H., Inequities, C. on the R. of F. P. that C. to R. and E. H., Geller, A. B., Polsky, D. E., & Burke, S. P. (2023, July 27). *Health Care Access and Quality*. Www.ncbi.nlm.nih.gov; National Academies Press (US). https://www.ncbi.nlm.nih.gov/books/NBK596397/

Simhoni, S. (2024). *Ensuring contraception options are accessible and affordable. Center for American Progress*. Retrieved from https://www.americanprogress.org/article/playbook-for-the-advancement-of-women-in-the-economy/ensuring-contraception-options-are-accessible-and-affordable/

Taylor, J. (2017). *How women would be hurt by ACA repeal and defunding of Planned Parenthood. Center for American Progress*. Retrieved from https://www.americanprogress.org/article/how-women-would-be-hurt-by-aca-repeal-and-defunding-of-planned-parenthood/

American Immigration Council. (2023, May 2). *Beyond A Border Solution*. American Immigration Council. https://www.americanimmigrationcouncil.org/research/beyond-border-solutions

Clardie, J. (2011). *The Impact of Military Spending on the Likelihood of Democratic Transition Failure: Testing Two Competing Theories*. Armed Forces & Society. https://www.jstor.org/stable/48609093

Leading by Example: US Refugee Policy at Home and Abroad | Wilson Center. (n.d.). Www.wilsoncenter.org. https://www.wilsoncenter.org/article/leading-example-us-refugee-policy-home-and-abroad

Lopes da Silva, D. (2022, October 8). *Political Accountability and Military Spending*. Defence and Peace Economics. https://doi.org/10.1080/10242694.2022.2129128

Lee, N. T., & Chin, C. (2022, April 12). *Police Surveillance and Facial Recognition: Why Data Privacy Is Imperative for Communities of Color*. Brookings. https://www.brookings.edu/articles/police-surveillance-and-facial-recognition-why-data-privacy-is-an-imperative-for-communities-of-color/

Murray, D., Fussey, P., Hove, K., Wairagala Wakabi, Kimumwe, P., Saki, O., & Stevens, A. (2023, July 31). *The Chilling Effects of Surveillance and Human Rights: Insights from Qualitative Research in Uganda and Zimbabwe*. Journal of Human Rights Practice; Oxford University Press. https://doi.org/10.1093/jhuman/huad020

Wasem, R. E. (2020, September). *More than a Wall: The Rise and Fall of US Asylum and Refugee Policy*. Journal on Migration and Human Security. https://doi.org/10.1177/2331502420948847

Chapman, N., & Yoshino, K. (2023). *Interpretation: The Fourteenth Amendment Due Process Clause | Constitution Center*. National Constitution Center. https://constitutioncenter.org/the-constitution/articles/amendment-xiv/clauses/701

Simon, C. A., Steel, B. S., & Lovrich, N. P. (2018). *Chapter 2: Federalism*. Open.oregonstate.education; Oregon State University. https://open.oregonstate.education/government/chapter/chapter-2/

States' Rights--and Wrongs. (n.d.). Hoover Institution. https://www.hoover.org/research/states-rights-and-wrongs

Thurman, T. (2023, December 11). *Federalism.* American Cornerstone Institute. https://americancornerstone.org/federalism/

United States Courts. (2023). *Supreme Court Landmarks.* United States Courts. https://www.uscourts.gov/about-federal-courts/educational-resources/supreme-court-landmarks

What Movements Do to Law. (n.d.). Boston Review. https://www.bostonreview.net/articles/what-movements-do-to-law/

ACLU. (2023, October 6). *Why Access to Voting is Key to Systemic Equality | ACLU.* American Civil Liberties Union. https://www.aclu.org/news/voting-rights/why-access-to-voting-is-key-to-systemic-equality

Brennan Center for Justice. (2022, January 10). *The Impact of Voter Suppression on Communities of Color | Brennan Center for Justice.* Www.brennancenter.org; Brennan Center for Justice. https://www.brennancenter.org/our-work/research-reports/impact-voter-suppression-communities-color

Hesano, D. (2023, November 16). *How ID Requirements Harm Marginalized Communities and Their Right to Vote.* Democracy Docket. https://www.democracydocket.com/analysis/how-id-requirements-harm-marginalized-communities-and-their-right-to-vote/

Ian Vandewalker. (2020, September 2). *Digital Disinformation and Vote Suppression | Brennan Center for Justice.* Www.brennancenter.org. https://www.brennancenter.org/our-work/research-reports/digital-disinformation-and-vote-suppression

Kirschenbaum, J., & Li, M. (2021, August 10). *Gerrymandering Explained.* Www.brennancenter.org; Brennan Center for Justice. https://www.brennancenter.org/our-work/research-reports/gerrymandering-explained

Root, D., & Ives-Rublee, M. (2021). *Enhancing Accessibility in U.S. Elections.* Center for American Progress. https://www.americanprogress.org/article/enhancing-accessibility-u-s-elections/

Solomon, D., Maxwell, C., & Castro, A. (2019, August 7). *Systematic Inequality and American Democracy.* Center for American Progress; Center for American Progress. https://www.americanprogress.org/article/systematic-inequality-american-democracy/

Tausanovitch, A. (2019, October 1). *The Impact of Partisan Gerrymandering.* Center for American Progress. https://www.americanprogress.org/article/impact-partisan-gerrymandering/

5 Ways Secret Money Makes Its Way into Our Elections. (2022, October 11). Campaign Legal Center. https://campaignlegal.org/update/5-ways-secret-money-makes-its-way-our-elections

Craig, J., & Madland, D. (2014, May 2). *How Campaign Contributions and Lobbying Can Lead to Inefficient Economic Policy.* Center for American Progress. https://www.americanprogress.org/article/how-campaign-contributions-and-lobbying-can-lead-to-inefficient-economic-policy/

Dark Money Basics. (2016). OpenSecrets. https://www.opensecrets.org/dark-money/basics

Kennedy, L., & Root, D. (2017, April 27). *Trump at 100 Days: Case Studies of Trump's Self-Serving, Special Interest Government.* Center for American Progress. https://www.americanprogress.org/article/trump-100-days-case-studies-trumps-self-serving-special-interest-government/

Lobbying and Political Activities | Emory University | Atlanta GA. (n.d.). Staging.web.emory.edu. https://finance.emory.edu/home/financedivision/accounting/tax/lobbying-political-activities.html

Nazur, F. J. (2022, February 6). *Corporate Influence: Exploring the Relationship Between Lobbying and Corporate Power.* Harvard Law School | Systemic Justice Project. https://systemicjustice.org/article/corporate-influence/

Project 2025, Explained | American Civil Liberties Union. (2024, August 14). American Civil Liberties Union. https://www.aclu.org/project-2025-explained

The People's Guide to Project 2025. (n.d.). Democracy Forward. https://democracyforward.org/the-peoples-guide-to-project-2025/

CBPP. (2024). *House republican agendas and Project 2025 would increase poverty and hardship, drive up the uninsured rate, and disinvest people, communities, and the economy. Center on Budget and Policy Priorities.* Retrieved from https://www.cbpp.org/research/federal-budget/house-republican-agendas-and-project-2025-would-increase-poverty-and

Election 2024: Exposing Project 2025 | GLAAD. (2024, June 24). Glaad.org. https://glaad.org/election-2024-exposing-project-2025/

Johns, M., & Rosenthal, J. (2022, May 17). *How Investing in Public Health Will Strengthen America's Health*. Center for American Progress. https://www.americanprogress.org/article/how-investing-in-public-health-will-strengthen-americas-health/

Steele, J. B. (2022, November 29). *How four decades of tax cuts fueled inequality*. Center for Public Integrity. https://publicintegrity.org/inequality-poverty-opportunity/taxes/unequal-burden/how-four-decades-of-tax-cuts-fueled-inequality/

Schermerhorn, C. (2023, December 4). *History Explains the Racial Wealth Gap*. Time. https://time.com/6334291/racial-wealth-gap-reagan-history/

Tensley, B. (2024, April 25). *"Project 2025" and the Movement That Could Erode Black Equality*. Capital B News. https://capitalbnews.org/project-2025-black-voters/

What is Project 2025 and what does it mean for LGBTQ Americans? (n.d.). Www.advocate.com. https://www.advocate.com/politics/project-2025-anti-lgbtq

Carson, A., & Gibbons, A. (2023, May 3). *The Big Chill? How Journalists and Sources Perceive and Respond to Fake News Laws in Indonesia and Singapore*. Journalism Studies. https://doi.org/10.1080/1461670x.2023.2192299

Huang, X. (2024, April 4). *Silencing the Truth: The Global Crisis of Press Freedom and Journalist Safety*. Human Rights First. https://humanrightsfirst.org/library/silencing-the-truth-the-global-crisis-of-press-freedom-and-journalist-safety/

Levinson-Waldman, R., Panduranga, H., & Patel, F. (2022, January 7). *Social Media Surveillance by the U.S. Government*. Brennan Center for Justice. https://www.brennancenter.org/our-work/research-reports/social-media-surveillance-us-government

Media, L. (2023). *Building a Stronger Local Media Ecosystem: The Role of Media Policy*. Columbia Journalism Review. https://www.cjr.org/tow_center_reports/building-a-stronger-local-media-ecosystem-the-role-of-media-policy.php/

The Evolution of Authoritarian Digital Influence: Grappling with the New Normal. (2020, October 21). Sixteenth Air Force (Air Forces Cyber). https://www.16af.af.mil/Newsroom/Article-Display/Article/2389118/the-evolution-of-authoritarian-digital-influence-grappling-with-the-new-normal/

The Rise of Digital Authoritarianism: Fake news, data collection and the challenge to democracy. (2018, November). Freedomhouse.org. https://freedomhouse.org/article/rise-digital-authoritarianism-fake-news-data-collection-and-challenge-democracy

United States Department of State. (2022). *2f989377f9*. Retrieved from https://www.state.gov/report/custom/2f989377f9-3/

Bias on the bench. (2019). Aeaweb.org. https://www.aeaweb.org/research/federal-judicial-appointments-politics-impact-sentencing-decisions

Bazelon, E. (2024, April 29). *How "History and Tradition" Rulings Are Changing American Law*. The New York Times. https://www.nytimes.com/2024/04/29/magazine/history-tradition-law-conservative-judges.html

Conservatives and the Court. (n.d.). Www.nationalaffairs.com. https://www.nationalaffairs.com/publications/detail/conservatives-and-the-court

Justice: Open Justice. (2022, September 13). Open Government Partnership. https://www.opengovpartnership.org/open-gov-guide/justice-open-justice/

Root, D., & Berger, S. (2019, May 8). *Structural Reforms to the Federal Judiciary*. Center for American Progress. https://www.americanprogress.org/article/structural-reforms-federal-judiciary/

United States Courts. (2019). *Federal Courts & the Public*. United States Courts. https://www.uscourts.gov/about-federal-courts/federal-courts-public

Buckley, S. (2016). *Advocacy strategies and approaches: Overview | Association for Progressive Communications*. Apc.org. https://www.apc.org/en/advocacy-strategies-and-approaches-overview

Community Stakeholder Collaboration: A Key to Social Justice. (2024, April 30). Team Collaboration, Work Effectiveness & Creativity Tips | Futuramo Blog. https://futuramo.com/blog/the-importance-of-community-stakeholder-collaboration-for-improving-society/

Grasstops vs Grassroots Advocacy. (2023). Thecampaignworkshop.com. https://www.thecampaignworkshop.com/blog/advocacy-campaigns/grassroots-advocacy

NW, 1615 L. S., Suite 800Washington, & Inquiries, D. 20036USA202-419-4300 | M.-8.-8. | F.-4.-4. | M. (2021, February 18). *Worries about life in 2025*. Pew Research Center: Internet, Science & Tech. https://www.pewresearch.org/internet/2021/02/18/worries-about-life-in-2025/

Rector, K. (2024, July 14). *Project 2025, GOP platform blast California, teeing up critiques of Biden stand-ins*. Los Angeles Times; Los Angeles Times. https://www.latimes.com/politics/story/2024-07-14/under-project-2025-or-the-gop-platform-a-trump-win-will-mean-federal-war-on-california

Reid, A., Abraczinskas, M., Scott, V., Stanzler, M., Parry, G., Scaccia, J., Wandersman, A., & Ramaswamy, R. (2019, April 13). *Using collaborative coalition processes to advance community health, well-being, and equity: A multiple–case study analysis from a national community transformation initiative*. Health Education & Behavior. https://doi.org/10.1177/1090198119838833

Wagner, P. M., Ocelík, P., Gronow, A., Ylä-Anttila, T., & Metz, F. (2023, January 6). *Challenging the insider-outsider approach to advocacy: how collaboration networks and belief similarities shape strategy choices*. Policy & Politics. https://doi.org/10.1332/030557322x16681603168232

Aristotle. (2023). *Amplify your voice: Using social media to promote grassroots activism. Aristotle Blog*. Retrieved from https://www.aristotle.com/blog/2023/12/amplify-your-voice-using-social-media-to-promote-grassroots-activism/

Bettencourt, A. (2019, January 12). *Grassroots organizations are just as important as seed money for innovation*. UNHCR Innovation; UNHCR. https://www.unhcr.org/innovation/grassroots-organizations-are-just-as-important-as-seed-money-for-innovation/

Canelo, K. S. (2019, November 27). *State Coalitions, Informational Signals, and Success as Amicus Curiae at the U.S. Supreme Court*. State Politics & Policy Quarterly. https://doi.org/10.1177/1532440019889372

Effects of Shelby County v. Holder on the Voting Rights Act | Brennan Center for Justice. (2023, June 23). Www.brennancenter.org. https://www.brennancenter.org/our-work/research-reports/effects-shelby-county-v-holder-voting-rights-act

Grassroots Advocacy Strategies for Corporate Public Affairs. (2023, August 11). Bloomberg Government. https://about.bgov.com/brief/grassroots-advocacy-strategies-for-corporate-public-affairs/

Legal Action Center. (2019). Legal Action Center. https://www.lac.org/work/what-we-do/coalitions-and-collaboration

Landmark Civil Rights Cases Decided by the Supreme Court. (n.d.). The American College of Trust and Estate Counsel. https://www.actec.org/resource-center/video/landmark-civil-rights-cases-decided-by-the-supreme-court/

Leaders, A. (2014). *Public Rights Project*. Public Rights Project. https://www.publicrightsproject.org/alf12345

Public Interest Law | Georgetown Law. (2024). Georgetown Law. https://curriculum.law.georgetown.edu/jd/public-interest-law/

Albrecht, P., Patey, L., Abrahamsen, R., & Williams, P. D. (2024, May 7). *From peacekeeping missions to global peacekeeping assemblages*. International Affairs; Oxford University Press. https://doi.org/10.1093/ia/iiae064

Blitzer, J. (2024, July 15). *Inside the Trump Plan for 2025*. The New Yorker. https://www.newyorker.com/magazine/2024/07/22/inside-the-trump-plan-for-2025

Harrison, D. (2024, July 16). *Trump's Environmental Impact Endures, at Home and Around the World*. Inside Climate News. https://insideclimatenews.org/news/16072024/trump-environmental-impact/

Rodriguez, C. (2024). *Project 2025: The plan to seize power by gutting America's system of checks and balances. Center for American Progress*. Retrieved from https://www.americanprogress.org/article/project-2025-the-plan-to-seize-power-by-gutting-americas-system-of-checks-and-balances/

Strategic Change in U.S. Foreign Policy. (2024). Carnegieendowment.org. https://carnegieendowment.org/research/2024/07/strategic-change-us-foreign-policy

Sall, L., & Gross, S. (2024, July 30). *Trump has big plans for climate and energy policy, but can he implement them?* Brookings. https://www.brookings.edu/articles/trump-has-big-plans-for-climate-and-energy-policy-but-can-he-implement-them/

US department of state. (2022, April 1). *United States Strategy to Prevent Conflict and Promote Stability*. United States Department of State. https://www.state.gov/united-states-strategy-to-prevent-conflict-and-promote-stability/

Unmasking the Anti-Democracy Agenda of Project 2025. (2024, July 18). Democracy Docket. https://www.democracydocket.com/analysis/unmasking-the-anti-democracy-agenda-of-project-2025/

Involving Youth in Positive Youth Development | Youth.gov. (n.d.). Youth.gov. https://youth.gov/youth-topics/involving-youth-positive-youth-development

Mike, C. (2023, October 16). *The Benefits of Debate and Public Speaking Training for Kids*. Learningleaders.com; LearningLeaders, Inc. https://www.learningleaders.com/insights/the-benefits-of-debate-and-public-speaking-training-for-kids

Patel, K. (2024, August 7). *Media Literacy Guide: Empowering Youth in the Digital Age*. Octane Seating. https://octaneseating.com/blog/media-literacy-education

Schulten, K. (2022, October 20). *Teenagers and Misinformation: Some Starting Points for Teaching Media Literacy*. The New York Times. https://www.nytimes.com/2022/10/20/learning/lesson-plans/teenagers-and-misinformation-some-starting-points-for-teaching-media-literacy.html

Soken-Huberty, E. (2020, May 16). *What is Social Justice in Education?* Human Rights Careers. https://www.humanrightscareers.com/issues/what-is-social-justice-in-education/

The Benefits of Public Speaking and Debating Skills for Academic Success. (n.d.). Www.learningleaders.com. https://www.learningleaders.com/insights/the-benefits-of-public-speaking-and-debating-skills-for-academic-success

Winthrop, R. (2020, June 4). *The need for civic education in 21st-century schools*. Brookings; Brookings. https://www.brookings.edu/articles/the-need-for-civic-education-in-21st-century-schools/

youth. GOV. (2019). *Civic Engagement | Youth.gov*. Youth.gov. https://youth.gov/youth-topics/civic-engagement-and-volunteering

Made in the USA
Las Vegas, NV
23 November 2024